The Cliff Dancer:
My Love Affair with Ivan Dixon

Written by Bettina E. Washington

&

Fatima Washington

DEDICATION

This book is dedicated to any woman who would fall in love with a married man.
Run. Don't walk. You are on sacred ground.

ACKNOWLEDGEMENTS

This book could not have come together without our editor, Ryan Graff. Our heartfelt thanks also to Corey Johnson, who was there from the beginning, Dion Fearon, a constant and honest sounding board, Igbo Obioha, our attorney and friend, Loretta Eves and our family the Washington clan...past, present and future. We stand on your shoulders.

CONTENTS

PROLOGUE - 1967

My hand shook as I pointed my .22 caliber gun at my husband. My voice was much calmer than I felt when I told him, "I don't want any problems. The attorney is waiting for us to come and sign the papers together; no more missing appointments. So get your jacket and let's go."

George just stared at me. He said nothing, and did exactly what he was told. Grabbing his jacket, he walked in front of me and proceeded towards my two-door Coupe de Ville Cadillac. On any other day, I might've taken a moment to admire the gleaming white exterior and all-black leather interior. That day, all I cared about was getting his ass in the passenger seat.

15 years ago, I'd never have dreamed that I'd ever point a gun at this man. The man I'd vowed to love and respect 'til death do us part. The man for whom I'd borne three children, and the man who'd been cheating on me from the day I'd first given him everything. George might have thought I was crazy for coming to

his dental office armed. Maybe I was and maybe I wasn't, but he was the crazy one if he thought I was going to put up with his cheating ways for one more day.

With my left hand, I drove down Crenshaw Boulevard at a moderate 35 mph. With my right hand, I kept the gun raised and ready. George could only stare at me, part in amazement and part in terror. I could only imagine what was going on in his head, but that was the least of my concerns. I was a woman on a mission, willing and able to pull the trigger. If he'd given me the slightest excuse, that would have been it for him right there – no hesitation, no regrets, and no sympathy.

As we turned into the parking lot of my attorney's office, I took one last look at the man I no longer loved. He felt like a stranger, someone who had slowly and methodically forced the love out of our lives and replaced it with hate, anger, and disgust.

George tried to say something, but I stopped him in his tracks.

"I don't need to hear anything you have to say. You're the scum of the earth. If I never did anything for you, you can believe that I never will again."

George looked away. I was done with him, had been for years, and I think that was the moment he finally understood.

Yes, that part of my life was finally over, and I was free to begin a life I so longed to live. A life with a man who knew the meaning of love, honor, and respect. A life with a man who knew how to love me for who I was, regardless of my issues – *all* my issues. A life with a man I now call my soulmate. A man named

Ivan Dixon.

I'd been in love with Ivan since the second I saw him in the movie *A Raisin in the Sun*. The day I saw that movie changed my life, and over time, it made me into the person I am today. It happened in a blink of an eye, and lasted for what felt like a lifetime. Our love affair was birthed by fate, only to be tested in an encounter with Christ. It would tear me apart as it inevitably forced me to choose between my soulmate Ivan and my conscience.

It hasn't always been an easy story to understand — not even for me, and I lived through it. The best way to make sense of it is to start at the beginning, all the way back in my early childhood.

This is my story.

CHAPTER 1 - 1933

I was an only child, raised by my father's mother. My real mother didn't raise me; she was only 15 when she had me. My mother didn't know anything about raising babies. She was footloose and fancy free and was more concerned with dancing 'til the wee hours of the night than with breastfeeding or diapers.

My daddy had no business taking care of a baby on his own either. As a working musician and professional saxophone player in Baltimore, he played gigs all around town with famous band leaders like Jimmie Lunceford and Andy Kirk. He even went on the road with his famous sister, Wee Bea Booze, also known as "The See See Rider Blues Girl." Aunt Muriel was a popular jazz vocalist and guitar player, signed to Decca Records, and in 1942, her version of Ma Rainey's song "See See Rider" shot to #1 on the "Harlem Hit Parade" charts. Later, Elvis Presley would make that song popular the world over by performing it in his concerts until the day he died.

When my daddy wasn't on the road playing gigs with Aunt Muriel, he was working late nights and sleeping during the day. At least he had enough sense to know I needed a stable home. He was fed up with my mother leaving me with different family members each night so she could go out and dance, and he knew he couldn't do much better for me himself. So when I was three years old, my daddy took me to live with his mother, my Grandma Lydia.

My daddy delivered me to my Grandmother's doorstep like a stork, saying, "Here, Mama, her mama either can't or won't take care of my baby."

My Grandma Lydia was considered the matriarch of the family. A strong woman and devout Methodist, she always kept me in awe. For years, I thought she was a giant, towering over everyone in our family. Of course, as I grew up, I found out that she was barely five feet tall, hiding her 4'-11" petite frame under layers of worn-out clothes.

During the day, she worked as a maid, cleaning homes for rich people who didn't even know her name and didn't care to learn it. She had high cheekbones and small eyes that complimented her perfectly proportioned face on her ebony black skin. In those days, being dark was not considered beautiful, and Grandma Lydia was very, very dark. Nonetheless, people called her attractive, so much so that she never needed to wear any makeup.

At that point, I didn't have any memories of my real mother. I thought Grandma Lydia *was* my mother for a long time, and so I called her mama, which fit me just fine. In fact, for many years, I thought I had two fathers: My grandfather Philip, whom I called "Papa" and my father, whom I called "Daddy."

It wasn't until I was seven years old that I was able to remember bits and pieces of my childhood. What stood out the most was where we lived. We had a typical three-story Baltimore row house. In front was a concrete porch, with two steps and plenty of room for us to sit outside during the hot summer nights. Most houses in Baltimore were brick row homes, and ours wasn't any different.

Our second-floor bedroom was converted into a kitchen. Everything took place in that one room, and I mean everything. From breakfast to dinner and socializing — we would even hold everyone's Saturday night baths there.

My bed was a small cot beside a larger bed in the room where Grandma Lydia and "Papa" Philip slept. The room was stuffed with dresses, folded clothes, blankets, and other small beds. We had access to the other parts of the house, but Grandma Lydia kept everything in that main room, especially the heat, so that's where we all stayed.

Our house was never empty; I, as the only child, lived with great-grandparents, grandparents, great aunts, great uncles, aunts, second cousins, and my father. We even had mice and roaches too. No one seemed to think twice while the vermin scurried across the floor; we just carried on with our lives. They seemed to know their way around the house just as well as we did.

We didn't have the luxuries that other people had, like a telephone, refrigerator, or even a gas stove. We were unquestionably poor. While we had electricity, my grandmother preferred to burn kerosene lamps. For a while, I didn't know just how poor we were, because I was never allowed to go to other people's homes. Of course, they couldn't keep me away from everyone else in the world forever, and once I saw how other people lived, I wanted to leave my crowded, shoddy home as fast as possible.

On my ninth birthday, I found out my grandmother was not truly my mother.

My real mother came over that day, with a coconut cake in her hands. I remember the moment clearly when my grandmother looked at me and said, "This is your mother. I'm not your mother. I'm your grandmother."

I stared blankly at the woman they said was my mother. She wasn't much taller than Grandma Lydia. She was brown skinned, not dark, with dark brown shoulder-length hair framing an attractive face. She didn't say much to me; she only sort of looked at me while she handed me my birthday cake.

"Happy birthday, Betty," my mother said with a half-smile on her face. We held a stare. Neither of us moved from our designated spots.

I guess she was waiting for me to say something first. My Grandma Lydia nudged me, so I smiled and quietly said to her, "Thank you for the cake."

"You're welcome. I hope you like it. I heard coconut was your favorite," she said with a little pep in her speech.

I wanted to say *I don't know who told you that*, but Grandma Lydia taught me not to sass back to my elders.

"Yes, yes it is," I said, smiling and looking at Grandma Lydia.

It was a very strange feeling seeing my biological mother for the first time at nine years old. I never bonded with my mother, but it wasn't for lack of trying.

For a little while, I even tried to live with her. Then, one night, I woke to find her boyfriend standing over my bed, naked as the day he was born, singing, "I Dream of Jeanie with the Light Brown Hair."

He finished his song and grinned at me. "Now move over so Big Daddy can get into bed with you," he said.

I took one look at him and said, in the most convincing voice I could muster up as a nine-year-old girl, "If you touch me, my father and uncles said they will kill you."

Just as quick as those words fell from my lips, his grin fell right off his face. I guess he knew I was serious; he turned and walked out of my room, mumbling words I don't want to repeat under his breath.

The next morning, I packed my bags and left. I never told my mother why I left. I didn't think she would believe me. But I knew Grandma Lydia's house was where I belonged.

When I was 12, I started visiting my grandmother on my mother's side. Grandma Jelly was her name. She was a heavyset woman, and wasn't shy at telling me how she felt about how I looked.

I remember my very first visit like it was yesterday. I was sitting at her kitchen table, coloring in my book, while Grandma Jelly was preparing dinner. I noticed Grandma Jelly kept looking at me while she split her attention between me and the pots on the stove. She stopped what she was doing, walked over to me, and put her hands on her hips. I wasn't sure what was going on in that mind of hers, until she took a deep breath and said, "You'd be all right if you weren't so dark."

I looked down at my hand coloring and saw what she saw: Dark chocolate skin. I'd never given much thought about my skin color. I'd never even thought anything was wrong with my color until Grandma Jelly pointed it out. Her words stung like ten bees having their way with me on a hot summer day.

It was no secret that she didn't like dark-skinned females. In fact, Grandma Jelly blatantly favored light-skinned people over darker ones. Both my Uncle Benjamin and Arvell married light-skinned women, and Grandma Jelly loved those two daughter-in-laws. She hated Uncle Clarence's wife, who was unusually dark.

As the years went by, she would go on saying horrible things about my color. I didn't know it then, but her words had a way of seeping through the surface of my skin and into my soul.

Soon though, I was introduced to music, and it became my life. Music had a way of lifting me up and away from all my worries. I used to play the old Victrola in our living room on the first floor for hours at a time. I would listen to incredible voices like Billie Holiday, Dinah Washington, Arthur Prysock, and Billy Eckstine. My favorite song of all was "The Man I Love" by Billie Holiday. I would listen to that song over and over again.

I didn't realize it then, but my need to be loved – by anyone – began before I was old enough to know better. Eventually, I found that love, but far too late for it to save me from the turmoil and pain I had to live through.

Me sitting on the stoop on Division Street, Baltimore, Maryland.

My aunt Muriel Booze, aka Wea Bea Booze, a singer and musician.

My mother, Grace Wesson. Her early years.

My mother, Grace Wesson.

My father, Alfred Booze and I in Baltimore. He was a local and well known

saxophone player.

With my dad, Alfred Booze. He always had a cigar or a saxophone in his hand. Although he was rarely home, he made sure his mother looked after me.

CHAPTER 2 - PIMLICO

When I turned 16, I met the man I would marry. His name was George Washington, and we were as opposite as they come. I was living in poverty and had an eighth grade education, and then there was George.

George was a World War II veteran, a college student, and star basketball player for Morgan State College at the time. He was tall, high yellow, and incredibly handsome. I was brown skinned, and while I was considered an attractive girl, the stigmatism that followed me with my skin being so dark created an insecurity that stayed with me through most of my life. So when I met George on the corner of Druid Hill Avenue on that hot and humid summer day, I never thought in a million years he would ever be interested in a girl like me.

George's brother Ernest was the one who introduced himself to me while I was waiting to catch the 38 bus. Ernest was the more outgoing of the two. He was also shorter and browner than George, but none of that really mattered to me at the time. Our first meeting was brief. I saw them a few feet away, getting out of their black Buick and heading over to where I was standing. I looked away, unsure if I was their intended target, but when Ernest came over to me with a smile, I figured it out fairly quickly.

"Pardon me, aren't you Betty Booze?" Ernest asked.

"Yes." I answered.

"I'm told you can dance. I love to dance," Ernest said.

"I can move all right," I replied.

"Well, we're having a party in Pimlico. You ought to come by and bring a couple of your girlfriends."

I looked over at George, who wasn't saying much at all. In fact, he just stood there being handsome and letting Ernest do all the talking.

"I'm Ernest, but everyone calls me Monk. Let me introduce my brother, George."

"Pleased to make your acquaintance," George mumbled quickly.

I could tell they were both educated, and I found out later I was right; Ernest was a chemistry major, and George was studying biology.

"So, can we expect you at the party?" Ernest asked as my bus arrived.

I looked them both over and made a decision. "Sure, I'll even bring a few of my girlfriends."

"Great," Ernest said. "We'll see you then!" "Oh, we live in Pimlico. 5306 Denmore Avenue."

I said my goodbyes and jumped on my waiting bus. From my seat at the window, I watched as George and Ernest made their way back to their car, laughing and talking along the way. I thought about who I would take to the party, and immediately thought about my three best friends: Marlene, Doris and Harriet. None of them would ever pass up a great time. Doris and Marlene loved to eat, Harriet was the boozer of the group, and I loved to dance, so we'd all have a good time.

That evening, I took a detour to my Uncle Clarence's house, since he had a telephone, and I got an excited "Yes" out of all three girls. Pimlico was a very far bus ride from downtown Baltimore, but that wasn't a problem; the only problem I foresaw was that the bus would stop running at midnight. We'd have to be well on our way home before then.

*****

The girls and I arrived at the party early. Ernest let us in at the door.

"Thank you for coming," Ernest said, beaming at us. "We have plenty of snacks, plenty to drink, so have as much as you want."

"Thanks," I said.

That was all my friends needed to hear; Harriet was off to the bar, and Marlene and Doris headed for the food. I had never seen so much food at one party. There were chips, onion rings, fried chicken, tuna salad, hard-boiled eggs, and lots of ham for us to eat. We quickly made sandwiches, thinking the food would be gone when the party got started. We shouldn't have worried; just like Ernest said, there was plenty all night.

Everything was going perfectly until 11 pm. That's when it all started to change. The tempo of the music downshifted, and someone swapped the light bulbs from white to blue and red. As the room grew dark, my gut went ice cold, and I knew nothing good was about to happen.

I turned to Marlene, who was still stuffing her face with the endless food, and said, "We need to get Doris and Harriet and get out of here now."

Marlene, Doris and I searched for Harriett in the dark house. It was a struggle, but we finally got Harriet away from the bar. With the last bus about to leave, all three of us ran out of the house, down the street, and caught it just in time. A minute more, and we would have been stuck out in Pimlico with no way to get home.

The next day, while visiting my Uncle Clarence, I saw Ernest and George pull up in their old black Buick. I assumed they were going to visit the physician's home next door, since his daughter was a very pretty, well-educated, high-yellow girl. But to my surprise, they ended up ringing my doorbell.

"Betty! Looks like you got yourself some visitors," the lady who owned the apartment yelled up to the second floor.

Curious, I headed downstairs and opened the door. "What do you want?" My tone made it clear that they were not exactly welcome.

"Betty," Ernest began, "you left before the party could even begin."

"I don't stay anywhere where I can't see two feet in front of me. Nothing good could ever come out of that," I said.

Ernest laughed, quickly picking up my tone. I'm not sure what he thought of me at that moment, but honestly, I didn't care. I looked over at George, who just stared at me, not saying a word.

Ernest continued, "I'll forgive you if you'll go to the beach tomorrow with my brother and me."

I thought for a minute, looking at Ernest, then at George again. I certainly didn't want to be the only girl going, so I thought I'd better bring a friend. "Well, I'd have to ask one of my girlfriends," I said.

"Yes, ask Marlene," Ernest eagerly suggested.

"Okay, I'll ask her."

George and Ernest turned to leave. George gave me one last look before heading out the door. In spite of everything so far, I actually liked him; I just wished he would talk a little bit more.

I shut the door behind me, then immediately went to the phone to call Marlene. She picked up the phone on the second ring.

"Hey Marlene, it's me, Betty. Ernest and his brother just left my house. They invited us to the beach with them tomorrow. Are you in, or—"

"Oh, count me in, definitely," Marlene said, stepping on my last few words.

"Be at my house tomorrow at 9 am."

"I'll be there," Marlene said eagerly.

The next morning, at 10 am, they picked us up in the old black Buick.

At first, I sat up front with Ernest, while George sat behind me, and Marlene sat next to him. With all the traffic that day, the drive was a long one, and Ernest spent it cracking jokes and talking about school. Marlene laughed at his jokes more than I did, while I found myself checking the rear view mirror, glancing back at George's face to see if he'd broken that stoic silence. By the time our feet hit the sand, Marlene was holding hands with Ernest, and I was hanging back with George. We spent the day walking and talking in the sun. Together at first, then Ernest and Marlene went on ahead, leaving George and me alone. Away from his brother, he finally started opening up.

"I saw you dance last night. How'd you learn to move like that?" George asked as we both sat down on a bench.

"I grew up in a musical home. There was always music being played. So what else are you gonna do but dance?" I said, smiling.

"Maybe you could teach me."

"Maybe," I said.

George and I spent the rest of the day talking and getting to know each other. Not only was George a pre-med student at Morgan State College, but he was also a basketball star. Even so, he had this quiet, humble way about him, almost as if he saw more in me than he did in himself. He made me so comfortable talking to him, I didn't even realize how strong my feelings were growing. Not so much romantic feelings; not at first. I just felt like I could trust George, like I finally had someone stable in my life.

After our trip to the beach, George and I hung out frequently, trying to see each other at least three or four times a week. Our friendship grew with every hour we spent together.

When we walked around together, people just stared at me. I imagined they were wondering who I was, since I didn't go to college. I didn't care what they thought; George and I were friends, and that was all that mattered.

George soon became my confidant. He was great at giving me advice on everything – even the guys I would date, like Lloyd Michener and Benjamin Hill. He said they were great guys, but he felt I could do better. I trusted George's opinion and took what he said to heart.

When I told Harriet about him, she just laughed and told me, "You know George likes you. Can't you see it?"

"George and I are just friends," I assured her.

It wasn't until we all went out to dinner, and George kept putting money in the jukebox to play the same song over and over again – Bull Moose Jackson; "You know I love you so/You know I'll never let you go" – that I really saw his fondness for me. George moved towards me and asked me to dance. As we moved together in rhythm on the dance floor, I could feel him hold me closer and closer. And then, just at the perfect moment, he kissed me.

I glanced over at Harriet, who was sitting at the table and laughing at me while she mouthed, "I told you so!"

We dated for two years, two years of laughs and tenderness and good company. Then, one night in my mother's bathroom, as I sat on his lap scratching the dandruff out of his hair, I took one loving look at him and said, "Let's get married."

"What did you say?" George asked, startled.

"Let's get married," I said again. "Everyone else is getting married, so let's get married too."

George sat there for a minute, not saying a word. Finally, he answered, "Well, let me think about it."

"How long do you need to think about it?"

George gave me a serious look, smiled and said, "About that long. Let's do it."

The next week, we headed to the Justice of the Peace to avoid spending any money. None of our parents were able to help us financially, so on February 11, 1950, George and I tied the knot in Towson, Maryland at the home of the Justice of the Peace and his wife.

We walked out of there like two little kids on a candy store-shopping spree.

"What did we just do?" George asked with a happy smile on his face.

"I think we just became man and wife, that's what I think," I replied happily.

Even though we were married, we continued to live apart in our separate family homes. Our plan was to announce our nuptials at the "right time," when we had a little bit socked away to have a proper wedding ceremony.

It took a few months, but eventually George's mother started sensing that something was different between us. George and his mother were exceptionally close, so it wasn't long before Mother Washington started to inquire, "Junior, you didn't go and get married, did you? You and Betty are too close."

George stood his ground. "No, Mother, we did not go and elope."

"Because if you did, I would be extremely disappointed," Mother Washington said to him, trying to use that innate power all mothers have to see if their sons are lying.

George never told his mother the truth about our marital status, no matter how hard she pushed. We were successful at keeping our nuptials a secret, though when my mother had a heart attack and George's mother had emergency surgery, we decided that we were going to have to get married all over again for everyone to see.

We set the date of our second wedding for June 24th, 1951. Of course, we could never reveal to our parents that we eloped, but we had to reveal the truth to my pastor, who surprisingly went along with the ruse. Of course, we were still just as broke as we had been, so I started looking out for ways to...*help fund* a proper wedding.

One day while I was preparing food for a big catering job with my part-time job at Bloomfield's Caterers, I saw an opportunity for some food and drink. I told George to come to my job at 3 pm and wait outside in the back by the bushes. While I prepared the sandwiches for the catering company, I would also make a few extra and drop them into a bag that sat between my legs under the table. George would smuggle the bags out back and stash them in his car. By the end of the night, I had over a three dozen ham and cheese sandwiches set aside for the wedding. This went on for a few days until we had enough sandwiches to feed fifty people.

The day before my wedding, I asked the owner for a wedding gift: A case of champagne, since I was getting married the next day.

He looked at me with a blank stare and said incredulously, "Absolutely not! You've been stealing food all week. Do you think I'm blind?"

I was ashamed and embarrassed, but at the end of the day, we had no money, so we did what we had to do. My manager never gave us that case of champagne, but our wedding was still very beautiful, and the sandwiches were delicious.

George and I decided to have our wedding at his mother's home in Pimlico, with all the trimmings. To avoid our parents finding out the truth about our eloping, my pastor had the regular marriage license filed with the certificate.

During our entire wedding ceremony, Mother Washington stood behind George, trying her best to see the writing on our marriage license. I wasn't going to let that happen. The second he pronounced us man and wife, I snatched the license right out of my pastor's hand, folded it, quickly shoved it down my bra, and kissed George. Our guests laughed, thinking I was an overanxious bride. Mother Washington never found out the truth.

George's parents, Rev. George Washington Sr. and Ethel Washington.

Mother Washington and her sons Ernest "Monk" Washington, George "Budddy" Washington and Joseph "Joe" Perry

Morgan Stage College Basketball Stars George Washington (#8) and Ernest

Washington (#19)

George and I on a date in Baltimore.

My graduation photo from Carver, which was a trade school in Baltimore.

Later, I would have to return to school as an adult and earn my high school

diploma at night.

Mother Washington.

My wedding in the backyard at the Washington's family home in Pimlico.

Later I would regret tearing it to pieces.

My Wedding Day, February 11, 1950.

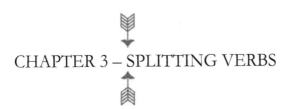

CHAPTER 3 – SPLITTING VERBS

In 1951, about a year after our "official" wedding, George and I moved to Washington, DC. I was eager to start a family, but to my dismay, a family was not on George's priority list, and he made that abundantly clear.

George graduated from Morgan State College, and though he was currently working as a medical technician, his ambition was to one day be a medical doctor. In DC, if your husband was studying to be part of the professional crowd, it was an open door to bourgeoisie society. Unfortunately, while "high society" certainly respected my husband's profession, I soon learned they didn't care for mine.

I was working as a clerk typist for the Washington, DC school system's probation department, with educated women who were all married to professional men. Some of the women there loved to talk over my head, or at least pretend to, not caring whether or not I understood their insults.

I thought I could grow to fit in with them, or at least shut them up, by pursuing a higher degree. I decided to attend night school at Howard University so I could earn my Bachelor's.

When I went to register for my classes, the clerk in Howard's admissions department told me flat-out with a smug look on her face, "You don't have a high school diploma." She piped up a bit, and almost sang the words, "You cannot enroll in any of the Bachelor's Degree programs."

I was utterly shocked and very much embarrassed. After doing some research into my education from Carver Vocational School, I found that graduating with a certificate in business training and cookery was not the same as a high school diploma. Carver focused more on trades and less on college prep, instead choosing to ready its all-colored graduating class to enter a post-World War II workforce with viable occupations like cosmetologists, clerk typists and mechanics. Needless to say, I was devastated, which amplified my already-present insecurities about my less-than-average educational background. I put my dreams of obtaining my Bachelor's degree on hold and looked for a way to obtain my high school diploma.

Meanwhile, for George, getting accepted into Howard University's medical program didn't come easily at all. He applied many times, but was greeted with multiple rejections. After the last rejection, George decided to go to dental school, took the dental entry examination, and hunkered down to wait for his results.

As fate would have it, things started falling into place for George and his medical future.

It started when Adelaide Hardy invited us to one of her parties. Adelaide worked in the same office as me, and was one of the few people there who liked me very much. She was a classy woman, with light brown shoulder length hair and graceful slim hands and fingers. Most people wouldn't call her pretty, but she had tons of class and always knew what to say, what to wear, and how to earn a friendship.

At the time, George's dental college application was still pending. Hoping I could help, I'd made an appointment with Dr. Dixon, the Dean of Howard University's Dental College. I had faith in my husband, and he thought I was crazy for trying to make the appointment in the first place. But to George's surprise, Dr. Dixon agreed to meet with me, on the Monday that happened to fall after the party.

Adelaide hosted the party at her house. She lived in an upscale neighborhood on the east side of town. Everyone there but me had some sort of college education; the majority of the people there were medical doctors, lawyers, or college professors. Neither George nor I knew any of them.

George didn't seem to mind that, and he managed to fit right in. I, on the other hand, felt out of place and terribly shy. To combat my insecurities, I fell back into a familiar role and began working as a caterer. I made little sandwiches, getting drinks for people and emptying ashtrays. In essence, I became the party's waitress. At one point, I was in such a zone that I didn't notice a man named Mr. Hayes tapping my hand. "Excuse me, would you kindly get me a drink, then come and sit with me?"

Mr. Hayes was the husband of a woman who worked in my department as a probation administrator. He was very short and wore glasses and his dark wavy black hair and mustache stood out against his light complexion. I returned with his drink, as ordered, set it next to him with a white napkin underneath, and sat down on the chair kitty-corner to him.

"What do you do?" Mr. Hayes asked as he slowly sipped on his drink.

"I'm a clerk typist at the school's probation department," I said, attempting to make myself feel more at ease.

"What about your husband over there?"

I smiled as I glanced over towards George, who was very much at ease with everyone around him, then quickly reverted my attention to Mr. Hayes. "Well, my husband's a medical technician. He's very educated, more so than me. I…" I looked around at all the fancy guests. "I don't usually come out to this kind of party."

Mr. Hayes gave me a reassuring nod and an understanding smile. "I remember when I first came here," he said. "You'll get used to the place if you stick around. They're nice people, once you get to know them." I felt myself relax a bit and ease into my chair. "So where are you from?" he added..

"We just moved here from Baltimore," I told him. "My husband is trying to get into the dental school at Howard University."

"Dental school at Howard," he said with a sip and a nod. "Tough admissions board there, you know."

"I know," I said. "That's why I have a plan."

"A plan?" Mr. Hayes asked, continuing to sip on his drink.

"I called the Dean himself, and made an appointment for Monday morning."

Mr. Hayes looked at me in amazement. He laughed. "And what do you plan on saying?"

I wasn't sure what was so humorous, but I continued anyway. "I'm going to tell him about how smart my husband is, and that we need help to get him into the school because we don't know any important people."

Mr. Hayes sat there with a smile on his face. Well, I thought, at least I was entertaining him.

"We don't have anybody to...you know, write a letter of recommendation or anything," I went on.

"Mrs. Washington, do you have a Howard University catalog?" Mr. Hayes asked in a nonchalant voice.

"Yes, I do."

"I would look through it, if I were you." he said.

"Why is that?" I asked.

"Humor me, please." Mr. Hayes said.

Mr. Hayes and I continued to chat. He never mentioned why he wanted me to look at the catalog, but I agreed that I would as soon as possible.

That night, when George and I returned home after the party, I was too tired to check the catalog. My only concern all weekend was my meeting with the Dean.

Monday finally came, and I headed to meet Dean Dixon. I still remember what I had on; I wore a brown tweed suit with an orange pillbox hat, Lizagator shoes, and a matching purse. My sharpest outfit for the most important meeting of my life thus far.

Compared to Dean Dixon's exceptionally large desk, he himself was a very unassuming man. He smiled at me when I entered his office, inviting me to take a seat across from him. My stomach clenched, but I ignored it and held my poise. I reminded myself that this was not the time to show my insecurities; it was time to stand up for my husband.

"Now, I already have your husband's examination records, but I want you to tell me about your husband yourself," Dean Dixon told me. He settled back in his large brown leather chair, as if he were waiting for his favorite movie to begin.

I reached in my bag and pulled out a neatly put together portfolio. First, I placed on Dean Dixon's desk George's transcripts from Morgan State College, as well as his grades from the Medical Technology College in Pennsylvania. Like a poker player revealing a winning hand, I kept adding all of George's achievements to the pile, including his basketball highlights, news write-ups about playing for Morgan State College, and his Kappa Alpha Psi fraternity membership. Lastly, I showed him how George was the first black in Baltimore to try out for the Baltimore Bullets.

Dr. Dixon didn't say a word. I tried my best to decipher his body language, but he had an excellent poker face. I placed the last of the paperwork in front of Dean Dixon; he didn't once glance down at it, but kept his eyes fixated on me.

He took a deep breath, then asked, "Mrs. Washington, do you understand what you are asking me to do?"

I just sort of looked at him. I wasn't sure if that was a rhetorical question or not; either way, I was at a loss for words. Before I had a chance to say anything, Dr. Dixon leaned forward in his chair, never once taking his stare off of me.

"We have over 1000 applicants each year looking to fill a small class of 20. So as you can see, the competition is high. I have mothers, fathers, grandparents, and *very* influential people who come into my office every day asking for favors." He leaned back and took another breath. "But I have to admit…this is the first time in my career that I ever had a wife with no influential backing or connections come into my office, making a case for her husband."

I listened to him go on, unsure of where he was going.

"So with that, Mrs. Washington…" he paused, grinned at me and said, "I am very impressed. George needs three votes from members on an admissions committee to get in. He has mine, and I will see what I can do about the other two, but I can't guarantee anything, you understand."

Hallelujah! I only remember grabbing him and saying over and over again, "Thank you! Thank you!"

I gathered my belongings and was about to leave when Dr. Dixon said to me, "Whatever you do, keep this to yourself. You can't tell your husband that I'm going to help him."

"I won't say a word. It'll be hard, but I won't. I promise. Thank you, thank you, thank you!"

I was on Cloud Nine while I headed home. I knew I had to keep my promise and not mention a word to George, and while it was going to be challenging, if it got him into dental school, I was all for it.

The next day, while relieving one of the switchboard secretaries at work at the probation department, I received a call from Mr. Hayes. I was surprised to hear his voice. Needless to say, I couldn't talk just then, with all the incoming calls flooding in. I quickly let him know I would call him back later that evening.

That evening, while I was preparing dinner, my phone rang. Once again, it was Mr. Hayes.

"How are you?" I asked with a smile.

"Mrs. Washington, I am by no means trying to be a pest, but I was calling to inquire if you had a chance to go through the catalogue."

With all the excitement over Dean Dixon, I had totally forgotten to look.

"Right, I haven't had chance, but I promise this evening after dinner, I'll look at it."

"Very well. Please phone me when you have."

"I will," I said.

"By the way, Betty, how was your appointment with Dean Dixon?"

"It went well, thank you." I didn't want to give Mr. Hayes too much detail until I knew something concrete.

"I'm glad to hear that. I look forward to your call, Betty."

That evening after dinner, I finally had a chance to look through the catalogue. While flipping through the pages, I was taken aback when I saw a picture of Mr. Hayes, with a caption reading, "*Dr. Hayes*, Head of Histology Department for the School of Dentistry."

My mouth and the catalogue hit the floor. "George!"

Together, we stared at the photograph.

"Is that who I think it is?" George asked, with as much amazement in his voice as there was in his expression.

"Yes, that's the gentleman from Adelaide's party, the one who was so nice to us both," I said, matching his excitement.

That next morning, I received two calls, one from Dr. Hayes and the second from Dr. Dixon. They both phoned with good news: George had their votes, and getting the third one shouldn't be a problem.

Dr. Dixon reminded me not to mention a thing about our conversation to George. "Let your husband be surprised when he receives his acceptance letters in the mail."

I told him I was still keeping my promise, and I did, though it got harder and harder over the next two weeks.

George finally received his acceptance letters, and he couldn't have been happier. When he opened them, he screamed so loudly I thought he was going to break something. I smiled with glee as he lifted me up from the floor and spun me around. George was delirious with happiness, and I couldn't have been more proud of him.

When people in the probation and psychology departments learned George was in his first year in dental college, the invitations began to roll in for us. All at once, the bourgeoisie community opened up their doors for him.

Him. Not me.

It didn't take long to learn that I still didn't fit in. Wherever we went, professionals and party guests welcomed George with open arms, but I'd be lucky if anyone asked me for a refill. Obviously, they looked down on my lack of education, but I did my best to grin and bear it for George's sake – until one particular party at Chesapeake Bay.

George and I accepted most of our invitations, and attended at least a party a week. After a while, they all started to run together, especially since I never knew anyone there. This one, though… This one I'd never forget.

George had been trying to push me into socializing more. "Don't be so shy," he'd tell me. "They'll love you once they get to know you." So, at the Chesapeake Bay party, I decided to give it a shot. There was a beautiful young woman from Jamaica there, with sparkling earrings and a sweet, lilting voice. Eloquent, too; not a native English speaker, but her accent made her more articulate somehow, and her stories brought laughs with every punchline.

I was a few feet away from her, drifting through the crowd in her direction, when I heard someone say, "She's a wonderful speaker, isn't she?"

I turned and said, "Yes, she does speak beautiful."

That's when I saw who I was talking to: A young lady in a long, expensive dress, who immediately raised her arms to announce, "You hear that?" She flicked her hand toward me. "She speaks beautiful!"

Everyone around me laughed. I didn't even know why. The lady leaned in and whispered, "You're beautiful, sweetie." She gave me a wink.

Another burst of laughs swirled all around me. I turned away and stared at the floor. I wanted to leave. I wanted to go home. I wanted to crawl off and die.

*****

"Beautiful," I said again to George as he stopped at a red light.

George shook his head and said, "Don't worry about it. That woman is stupid."

"Well, I don't know how stupid she could be if she attends Howard," I shot back. My head was swirling in confusion and anger. I hated that woman, hated all of them. Most of all, I hated that I'd given them the ammunition to mock me.

"Betty, she's just jealous. You have a husband. She doesn't. You're young. She's old."

"That woman couldn't have been but two years older than me." I said as I looked at George. He continued to drive, not looking my way. I could tell he was hiding something.

"Why don't you just tell me the truth?" I shouted.

"Fine, you used an adjective when you should have used an adverb."

"A what...? What's that?"

"Forget it, all right? Let's just drop the whole thing," George finally said as we pulled up to our apartment. He quickly jumped out of the car and headed toward the house. I didn't follow him right away; for a while, I sat in the car, alone. I couldn't believe what had happened, how I'd made a fool of myself.

At that moment, I vowed to never make a fool of myself again. I immediately enrolled in night classes at Cordoza High School, while still working both my day job and a second job on the weekends. In a little under two years, I received my high school diploma with the class of 1956.

Without skipping a beat, I decided to enroll in English Grammar 101 at Howard University's night school program. I was so adamant about speaking the "King's English" that I took English Grammar 102 at Howard University three times. When I attempted to enroll for another semester, the professor promptly informed me that I would not receive credit or a grade for the course. George thought I was crazy and wasting my time, but I didn't care; I would never make the same sort of mistakes with my grammar again.

That grammatical error had re-ignited my quest to get my college degree, and this time I was unstoppable. I grew hungry for everything academic, immersed myself in collegiate life, and even pledged the Alpha Kappa Alpha sorority on

Howard's campus. All in all, the whole "missing adverb"

fiasco turned out wonderful...ly.

My graduation photo from Cordoza High School. I would never break "the

King's English" again.

CHAPTER 4 – HUMPTY DUMPTY

In 1956, about two years into George's four-year stint in dental school, I started seeing a drastic change in our marriage. We had stopped attending church, and we were slowly forgetting our roots. While faith took a comfortable backseat, evil walked in the front door. The kind of evil that breaks down love and sets men's minds to wander.

For the first time, I suspected that George might be cheating.

I firmly believe that a wife is the first to know when her husband is cheating—whether we want to admit it to ourselves or not.

It started with calls coming into the house with no one on the other end. The moment I would walk through the door, George would abruptly end his phone calls. Soon after that, George's Friday and Saturday night "poker games" would end later and later. Before long, I knew exactly what was happening.

The knowledge of what he was doing wormed its way through my whole life, my whole body. I started getting constantly distracted, or suddenly angry. My attention span slipped away. I slept sporadically, getting less and less rest, and could barely bring myself to eat anything. I lost all kinds of weight, and not in a healthy way.

I knew I had to make a change; I just didn't know how. My pride and fear kept me silent. I never talked about our marital problems, and never once uttered a negative word about George or his distasteful ways. I didn't even confront George about any of it. All I did was suffer in silence, dying by degrees while trying to make sense of it all. Of course, something had to give eventually.

One weekend, on my day off, I drove to Pimlico to visit George's mother, who had been helping us out with food. Mother Washington took one look at me and said, "You're a good girl, and I don't know what my Junior is doing to you, but he's not worth it. You're going to die, and some other woman is going to come in and get what you've worked so hard for."

She was absolutely right. It was like she'd shined a spotlight right through the dark, straight at me. "...And not to mention you are a bag of bones," Mother Washington continued while looking me up and down. "Let's go buy you a new skirt."

When I stood, I saw myself in her long mahogany mirror. I noticed for the first time how my clothes were barely staying on my frail body, all held up with safety pins. I hadn't realized just how much weight I'd lost in such a short time. I was slowly killing myself, and George didn't give a damn.

*****

It wasn't until I got transferred to the school system's psychology department that my mental state began to change for the better. George was still being unfaithful, and I didn't expect that to change, so to help myself, I decided to take a more active role in my own life. With the help of my co-workers, I glamorized myself a bit. I'd hoped that would help lift the fog all around me, and fortunately, it did.

I also started looking for someone to turn to, someone I could tell about my failing relationship. One evening, at a social gathering with Washington DC's young black doctors, I met Dr. Jones. She was quite tall for a woman, and wore eyeglasses that framed her face wonderfully. As we spoke, I learned that she was also my Alpha Kappa Alpha sorority sister. She happened to be a psychiatrist, who had started frequenting these gatherings with her husband, a surgeon. God must have been looking out for me that night, because I was definitely more outgoing than my usual self. Dr. Jones and I struck up a conversation, and she intuitively gave me her card and offered her professional services if I ever wanted to talk in private. I had never thought about seeing a psychiatrist before, but the thought now lingered in the back of my mind.

In 1957, I found out I was pregnant with my first child. Being pregnant, working, *and* attending Howard University was too much for me, so I decided that

I had to quit school. From there, life started speeding up.

Shortly thereafter, George graduated from dental school. We welcomed the birth of our first daughter, Valerie, on September 25th, 1958. Then George's internship at Jersey City Medical Center began, and I ended up moving in with my in–laws so Mother Washington could help with Valerie. (It wasn't until years later that I found out that during George's internship, he had been having an ongoing affair with a registered nurse.)

I was desperate to get away from the East Coast. I was ready to wash my hands of all the old memories there. So when George told me we were moving to the West Coast, I couldn't have been more thrilled.

*****

Mother Washington asked to come to California with us. George was against that — partly, I'm sure, because he didn't want the extra set of eyes watching him and his devious ways. I told George's mother that she would be more than welcome to come.

That said, I did ask her who was going to take care of her husband, Reverend Washington. Her response was classic Ethel Washington: "He doesn't need me! You do."

And in fact, I did. We had grown quite close while living together, so much so that people often thought I was her daughter and George was her son-in-law. I followed her everywhere — to church, the grocery store, shopping. When I had Valerie, she insisted that I go back to work full time so she could take care of Valerie during the day.

I found out one day that she had secretly told George, "She doesn't even know who Humpty Dumpty is, son! Betty needs my help."

George would defend me by saying, "Mom, it's her baby, and she has to learn."

Some nights at her place, I would reach out for Valerie and discover that my baby was gone. Usually, I'd find her in Mother and Revered Washington's bedroom, sleeping peacefully where they had moved her bassinet. I could only laugh all the way back to bed, being thankful for a good night's sleep. Mother Washington was a wonderful, kind, and sweet woman. She really was the mother I had never had.

Unfortunately, she died suddenly in June of 1959, just a few months before she would have been able to join us in California. Valerie was just barely a year old.

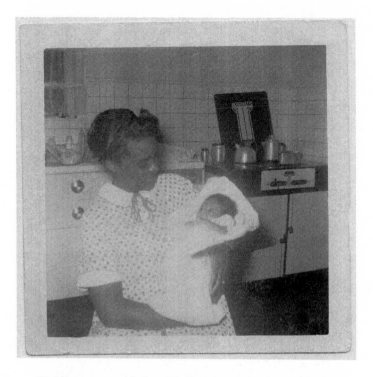

Holding my new baby girl, Valerie Elaine Washington.

Grandfather and granddaughter, Rev. Washington and Valerie in the backyard.

After Valerie's baptism in Maryland. George, Henry Brown, my grandfather,

Grace Wesson, my mother, me, Valerie, Rosetta Brown and Rev. Washington.

Ethel Washington, my mother-in-law and the mother I never had.

CHAPTER 5 – OUT OF THE FRYING PAN…

Soon after arriving in California, I became pregnant with our second child, Gregory. I was already working with the Department of the Navy as a clerk typist, while George stayed home studying with the kids until he passed his boards.

The day George passed the dental board, he called me at my job, telling me to quit right away and come home. I'd worked since I was fifteen years old, and had never walked off any job without giving proper notice. I told my boss about my situation, but promised to give the department two weeks' notice anyway. If my boss would let me leave early that day, I suggested, I could talk with my husband and convince him once his excitement subsided.

My boss seemed to delight in George's demand and said, "Mrs. Washington, when your husband becomes a doctor and tells you to quit your job and come home, you do it." I was stunned. He winked, waking me out of my daze, and added, "That's an order."

It was the first time in my adult life I had not worked. I thought that might make things different for myself and George, but before long, all the signs of our tumultuous life on the East Coast started to echo in the West. Los Angeles was no place for a married couple, especially a married couple with a husband who cheated at every turn of a skirt. I soon realized we had jumped out of the frying pan and into the fire.

The one thing that *was* different in California was the extravagant lifestyle we began to lead when George became a full-fledged, board-certified dentist. We started living the good life, as people would say.

I was no longer shopping at thrift stores and examining hand-me-downs for obvious tears. Instead, I was wearing the best fabrics of silk and wool from all the top designer labels like Oleg Cassini, Emilio Pucci, and Chanel. I even had a bottle of her infamous No. 5 Perfume. I got my nails done weekly at Saks Fifth Avenue and was known to wear my white cashmere coat out to social gatherings. We would eat at restaurants a few times a week, or else I'd prepare filet mignon, ground sirloin, shrimp, or lobster. George and I had never eaten so many rich foods in abundance in our entire lives. Because of that, I gained fifty pounds in our first few months of living there.

We soon found a cozy two-bedroom apartment in Los Angeles on Garthwaite Street, and quickly furnished it with all the best furniture money could buy for ourselves and our two children.

As a dentist's wife, I belonged to two important clubs: The Dental Wives, and the Medical, Dental, and Pharmaceutical Auxiliary Club. These clubs were not only our social outlets, with bridge, parties, and dances, but also great ways to help raise money for the NAACP and the United Negro College Fund.

I didn't know exactly what I was getting into, but I found out in short order. It wasn't long before evidence of George's rash of affairs began to surface, one after the other. It started with me discovering blood on George's shirt, from sleeping with a woman who was apparently on her period. Then there was the time George gave me a penicillin shot to cover up an STD he'd contracted and passed on to me.

I took the shirt to my friend Della. She was the wife of a former district attorney, and over time, she'd become like my adult play-mother. She looked at the shirt I brought her, called George a "dirty dog," and advised me on how to deal with his womanizing ways. "Betty, don't say anything," she told me. "Leave the shirt here with me. I'll burn it."

I let her burn the shirt, and said nothing to George.

All of his affairs were building up higher and higher. They were beyond hurtful. Soon, I felt as if I had nowhere to turn. I began to distance myself from George to keep my sanity intact, but inside, I was slowly coming undone, and I didn't know where that would lead.

The biggest blow came several months later, when I took my first trip to San Francisco with a sorority friend. I was only away for two nights. When I returned, George picked me up at the airport, and our 4-year-old daughter asked him,

"Daddy, are you going to pick up your red-headed girlfriend?"

George ignored Valerie, acting as if he didn't hear or understand what was coming out of our toddler's mouth, but I had heard her perfectly. Not long afterwards, I discovered red hair in my hairbrush, along with bobby pins behind our bed.

When I discovered that undeniable proof in our own bedroom, I hit my point of no return. I sat there frozen and stiff, silently internalizing my madness. It felt as if life, love, and everything good about my marriage had been drained out of me, drip by drip. My body lost all strength and coordination.

Days later, still lost in a haze, I made a decision to buy a gun.

*****

Now, I've made some bad decisions in my life, and buying a gun while angry was probably one of them. But by then, with all that George had put me through, buying one seemed perfectly reasonable.

I purchased a small revolver at Sears, complete with a permit to have it. The only thing I failed to do was learn how to shoot it properly. In retrospect, I suppose that's a good thing, because otherwise, I'd probably still be in jail.

Before long, I put that gun to good use. I started asking around about George's affairs. His secretary, who was almost as sick of his behavior as I was, let me know that the redhead he was sleeping with actually worked in his office. That was enough to get me moving.

The next morning, after dropping Gregory off at the babysitter and taking Valerie to nursery school, I turned around and headed for a certain spot on Western and Adams. George had mentioned a new "pharmacy" in the neighborhood, which his office had supposedly started using, but I knew better and followed my intuition. After circling a number of blocks, I saw George's car parked in front of an apartment building. I drove one block behind his car and waited for at least an hour before I finally saw him come out. George was carrying a TV, and there behind him was the redhead, dressed all in white.

Gritting my teeth, I slammed down on the gas pedal and crunched straight into George's rear bumper, pressing his car into the back of a parked milk truck. A glass milk bottle tipped out of the back and rolled over his hood. I tore open my car door, jumped out, grabbed the bottle, smashed it on the curb, and went after the redhead with the pointy end.

It's strange; I saw it all so clearly, but not from my own perspective, as if I were watching someone else do it. No; more like watching from outside my own body. Put another way, I'd snapped; I'd been pushed to my limit and it was time to make my anger, hurt and frustration known to all parties involved, especially to the woman who was screwing my husband.

George was too stunned to move. The redhead looked me in the eye for just long enough to scream, and kept screaming all the way back into the apartment. I followed her up the stairs and down the hallway. She barely managed to get through her door, slamming it behind her before I could get to her. Through the door, I heard her laughing – whether out of relief or just to mock me, I couldn't tell and didn't care.

I gave the door a good, solid kick, shaking the broken bottle in my hand. "I'll have something else for you next time," I said, "and you won't be able to run."

When I came stomping back out of the redhead's apartment building, George was still standing in the same spot, trying to calm a neighbor whose car I'd inadvertently blocked. He gave me a guilty look, like a dog who'd just peed on the carpet. I spat at him, got in my car, and drove away.

I went to the nursery school, picked up Valerie, and took her to my babysitter where Gregory was. I went home, dressed to kill, grabbed the gun, and loaded it. Not wanting any bystanders to get hurt, I called George's office and told the receptionist to leave when I got there. I gave my babysitter, Mama Jerry, everything she'd need to take care of business: Fifty dollars, the keys to my home, and my mother's address and phone number in Baltimore. I told her, "I may not be coming back."

She asked, "Mrs. Washington, what's wrong? You look wild."

I never answered her. All I remember after that is heading out of the house. I felt calm, determined, and most of all, righteous.

Slowly and carefully, I drove to George's office on Compton Boulevard. When I made my entrance, I swiveled my head over to the secretary and commanded her, "Leave now."

She didn't argue; she just stood up, grabbed her belongings, and bolted. I gave the same instructions to a patient in an exam room, removing the disposable bib from around her neck. I then slowly walked down the hall, toward the door with George's nameplate. There, I tore the door open, startling George at his desk.

He looked twice as startled when I pulled out the gun. "Where is she?"

George leaped to his feet, then froze, not knowing where to go or what to say. I heard footsteps coming down the hall. On a hunch, I turned and ran toward them. I didn't quite see whose they were, but I knew. I knew beyond all doubt.

I heard the door to the x-ray room snap shut. With a flash of a smile, I gripped the knob and turned the door. Inside, she knelt behind the screen, trembling like a child. She looked up at me, then down at the gun, and whimpered.

"I told you," I said, then raised the gun and took aim. Before I could pull the trigger, George knocked into me from behind, scrambling all over my back as he tried to grab the gun away. I tightened my grip on the gun, and as it waved around, I felt it jump in my hand as it went off again and again.

Most of the shots went wild, and three ended up in the door, but one clipped the redhead's leg as she tried to run. She shrieked and gushed out blood, but kept on running, stumbling past the two of us, escaping the room, and hobbling down the hall as fast as she could.

I finally slipped away from George, leaving him to fall on the floor. Looking down ahead of me, I saw a trail of blood, following the woman like red ants marching single file. The color of the blood matched the color of her cheaply

64

dyed hair. I followed that trail out into the hall, just in time to see her throw herself into a vacant office. She closed the heavy wooden door and locked it.

I pounded on the door. I don't remember what I said to her. The next thing I remember is George coming out of the x-ray room, wide-eyed and breathless, staring down the hall like he didn't know me.

In minutes the police were everywhere. I don't think I even heard the sirens; I just stood there, holding George's gaze, until a policeman's voice came from behind me. "Ma'am, please put down the gun."

I hesitated for just a moment, then sank down to one knee, lowered the gun to the floor, and brushed it aside. The policeman's partner picked it up and backed away with it. I saw George catch his breath and start to turn aside.

"Don't you go anywhere," that same policeman told him. "Ma'am, would you please come with me?"

Dr. Whitmore, who owned the building, was in the hallway. He directed the shaken redhead woman downstairs to remove the bullet, but not before we crossed eyes; I wanted to let her know I still meant business.

The policeman didn't put cuffs on me. He led me to the nearest open office – George's, as it happened – and closed the door. I saw his partner question a stammering George.

"Mrs. Washington, are you all right?" he asked me with a stern but comforting tone.

"I'm fine," I finally managed. "I didn't want to kill her. Just scare her."

George stared down at the floor, his face unreadable.

"I don't know what the hell just happened, but I have a pretty good idea." the policeman said, looking straight at George. "Seems to me your wife's gotten wind of those orgies you've been having here."

I hadn't, actually, but they didn't surprise me in the least. I glared at George, who still couldn't bring himself to look back at me.

"They're not..." he started, then mumbled something unintelligible.

"I'm sorry, what?" asked the policeman.

"They're not orgies," he finally got out.

"'Parties,' then," said the policeman. "Well, guess what, Dr. Washington? Here and now, they stop, and if I hear about any more of them, you *will* be arrested. Do you understand me?"

George nodded. I shook my head with the utmost disgust at the man I married.

The policeman snarled. "He's the one you should've shot, not her."

"Yes, I know," I said. The policeman couldn't help but smile at that.

I don't remember what else the policeman said, because I was too busy listening to the screams of the redhead downstairs. Twenty minutes later, after the screaming stopped, Dr. Whitmore knocked and let himself in. George glanced back in the direction of the screams, then shot him a quizzical look.

"What?" said Whitmore with a shrug. "You know we're low on anesthetic."

I grinned.

"Well, good news, Betty," Whitmore continued, "I convinced her not to press charges." The policeman nodded. I breathed a sigh of relief.

With an easy smile, Dr. Whitmore showed himself out, and the policeman focused back on the two of us. George still couldn't look my way.

"Mrs. Washington," the policeman asked, "how many children do you and Dr. Washington have?"

"We have two children."

He ordered George, "Give your wife some money."

George opened his desk's top drawer, pulled out his checkbook, scribbled something down, and handed a check to the policeman.

The policeman threw it right back at him. "What's she going to do with 50 dollars? Give her some real money, so she can properly take care of your children."

George tore up the check and started a new one. I hid a smile.

Finally, he tore the check out of his book and handed it to me. I looked down to see it made out for $250, which was a lot of money in the early sixties.

"Thank you, officer," I said. I didn't bother giving George a last look as I stood and headed out of the office.

I can't recall how I got home that day, but it was that night that I called my friend Della, who advised me to get a lawyer. I followed her advice, found a lawyer, and filed for legal separation from George. I changed the locks and gave him a half hour to come and get his clothes. I was slowly trying to close that chapter of my life, and while I knew it wouldn't be easy, I had taken the first few steps in the right direction.

What happened in that office might have been dangerous, might even have gotten someone killed, but no matter what happened, I would not have changed what I did for the world.

That said, I knew I needed to talk to someone. I remembered Dr. Jones, who'd given me her card a few years back, and gave her a call. To my surprise, not only did she remember me, but she and her husband had recently relocated from Washington D.C. to Los Angeles. What's meant to be will always find a way, right?

I made an appointment and drove to her office at Ross Medical Center. I didn't know why, but my body felt *tight*, with pressure all across my forehead. Perhaps subconsciously, I already knew I had bottled up my feelings too long. I didn't need a doctor to tell me that. I turned on the radio to calm my nerves. There was Ray Charles' voice, like honey on a bruise, singing his latest hit, "I Can't Stop Loving You."

During that first session, I unloaded like B-52 bomber. "I'm having a lot of crazy problems with my husband. I'm the mother *and* father to our children. He has no interaction with the kids. You know how most doctors work a half-day on Saturdays? He works a *full* day Saturday, and he's barely home on Sundays. There's no real communication. We don't talk. We have nothing in common. I've filed for legal separation. I just want out." I burst into tears.

Dr. Jones allowed me to let go and handed me a tissue. "You can only be mother to your children. You cannot play both roles. When you try to be both, then the children do not have a mother *or* a father. Betty, what made you stay with this man? He was playing around before you even left Washington."

"I don't have a degree. I don't have an education. I guess I'm afraid that I won't be able to take care of myself."

"How did he get through dental school?"

"His mother helped. I helped. I worked two jobs to put George through school. I gave up our apartment so he could use it for around-the-clock study groups. I practically lived in our bedroom! I cut his hair so we wouldn't spend money on a barber, and all my clothes, shoes and handbags were bought secondhand so we could save every penny. I even gave up my education for his."

"Then what makes you think you can't take care of yourself?"

Good question, and it stuck with me as I kept on seeing her.

George, Valerie and I in Los Angeles.

My new style makeover once on the West Coast.

On an outing to the park with the kids. Me, Gregory (in my arms) and Valerie.

Celebrating Halloween. Valerie and Gregory.

Gregory and Valerie in our home in Gardena, California.

Valerie at Christmastime at our home in California.

CHAPTER 6 – BETTY BANG BANG

A month passed before I even considered revisiting the real world. One Saturday afternoon, my good friend Della called. "The Dental Wives are having a dance at the Ambassador Hotel on Wilshire Boulevard. You need to come with me."

I took a deep breath. I wasn't interested in leaving the house. "I think I'll pass, Della," I heard myself say to her.

"Betty, you have to go to the dance, or you will never be able to hold your head up in Los Angeles. If you don't, all the men will be afraid of you," Della said. She was right; Della was rarely right about much, but this time, she was dead on.

I called Mama Jerry to babysit, picked out my favorite Oleg Cassini dress and my high heel shoes, and went to the Dental Wives' dance solo. Della and I arrived to the dance around 8:00 pm. The valet had plenty of cars parked up and down the street, so I knew the place would be packed. We walked through the massive

500-room swanky hotel – former home to the Academy Awards, Golden Globes and the Coconut Grove.

The Coconut Grove was the LA hotspot for live entertainment on the West Coast. Walking through the lobby, a person might cross paths with Nat King Cole, spot Frank Sinatra, or even shake hands with Sammy Davis Jr.

We made our way to the Ambassador Ballroom. As soon we entered, we were greeted with looks of total shock and disbelief – something I will never forget.

Yes, the medical society greeted me that night with faint smiles and cold shoulders – most of which came from the wives. I realized that even though the wives had very little to say to me, their husbands were quite friendly and cordial.

Della picked up on that same cold front. She nudged me, saying, "Don't pay them any attention. We're here to have fun and make a point. So let's get a drink."

After Della and I blew off the less-than-warm welcome and had that drink, we sat at a table near the back. Not long after we sat down, a dentist friend introduced me to a man by the name of John.

I wasn't interested in meeting anyone that night. Like I told Della, I was only there to show everyone I was not ashamed for what I had done.

I had to admit, though, that John was hard to ignore. He was tall, chocolate, and had an amazing smile. He was such a gentleman, too; a winning formula for any woman. We ended up spending the next two hours talking and getting to know each other. He kept asking me to dance, and I eventually gave in. But only for a dance; I wasn't going to be his date, or anyone else's for that matter. I was free, beholden to no one, for the first time in years, and I wasn't ready to give that up.

So I danced and danced, not just with him, but with several MDs and dentists that night. I loved music, and I wasn't afraid to show it. Many of the wives and ladies watched and whispered, but I tuned them out. All I heard was the music.

When the evening came to an end, John, being the gentleman that he was, walked me to my car. When we got there, John leaned against it, folded his arms, and smiled at me.

"I had a great time with you tonight, Betty."

"Same here, John."

"How would you like to have dinner with me next Saturday?"

I thought about it. Then, going against everything I set out not to do that night, I said, "Sure, that would be nice."

John reached into his jacket, pulled out a business card, and handed it to me. I took it and read it to myself. "Dr. John T. Wilson, M.D., Internist." I wasn't surprised that he was a doctor; it made perfect sense, considering the company I met him in.

"So I'll see you Saturday?" John asked with a smile. He planted a soft kiss on my cheek.

"Yes, I'll see you Saturday, John."

I drove home thinking about how nice the night I resisted turned out. Della was right; I had to show everyone I was not ashamed, and meeting John only verified that I was still in high demand.

The following Saturday rolled around faster than expected. I met John at a restaurant on Restaurant Row, La Cienega Boulevard. I have to admit, being out with John was a nice, refreshing change. He was a take-charge type of guy. With George, I'd been the one who'd had to remind the waiter or anyone else about anything. His passive nature had always extended to the household duties, too; I'd been in charge of bills, office expenses, and raising our children. In essence, I'd worn the pants.

But back to John. We took our seats, and right away, he started pouring on compliments. "You look very elegant tonight, Betty," he said with a smile. "You have such a regal look, something that makes people just want to stare at your beauty."

"Thank you."

The compliments were flattering, but they made me a bit uncomfortable, mainly because I felt John didn't really know who I was.

I smiled and stopped John from delivering his next compliment. "You know, John, I am not the woman you think I am."

John leaned forward a bit. "Is that so?"

I lowered my eyes a bit in shame. "A few months ago, I shot a woman. Tried to kill her. I didn't know how to shoot, so I only hit her in the leg. Luckily for me, she didn't press charges." I felt my heart beating a bit faster, not sure at how John would receive my insane confession.

John slid his hand across the table towards me, taking my left hand into his right. His hand felt rough and smooth at the same time, showing me that even though he was now a doctor, he'd had a lot of hard work in his past.

"Stop it. I know all about it." John looked away, then back at me, as if he was gathering the right words. "When you came through the door, several of the ladies said, 'Oh, look, here comes Betty Bang Bang!' The men understood why you did it, and they were proud of you for trying to protect your family. We don't ever have to mention it again."

I sat staring at John, because I had no idea there was so much gossip about me. Nevertheless, I felt my body relax. *Betty Bang Bang*, was it? I actually kind of liked that.

John and I dated for several months after that. He was a great distraction, and I liked him very much…but I was not in love with him.

George didn't make it easy to move on, especially since he continued to call me day and night, begging for a second chance, all during my courtship with John.

One evening, while I was cooking dinner in front of the kids, George called again.

"Betty, I know I messed up, but I do love you, and I promise if you give me one more chance, I will do right by you."

I couldn't say too much, since I didn't want the kids to know who it was on the line. "I gave you a chance, and you didn't care. Please do not call me anymore. Goodbye."

But every night, he would call back and plead his case again and again. He called me for five nights straight, each time with a "better" reason for me to forgive him. I was sure his desperation had a lot to do with the fact I was dating John, but to be honest, it was getting harder for me to say no; after all, George and I had years of history and shared two children together.

I finally introduced John to Gregory and Valerie, and John eventually began to include them in our dates together. Valerie seemed to take it in stride, but Gregory never got used to having John around, and he would question John at every turn.

"Do you know my daddy?" Gregory would ask, looking up at John.

"I do know your daddy." John answered with a smile.

"What's his name, then?"

"George is his name."

"No, it's not. It's Daddy!" Gregory said, laughing out loud.

John and I would just look and smile at each other. It was something that drove both of us crazy.

My relationship with John moved pretty quickly, and much too soon, he took us to the same restaurant where we'd had our first date, told me all about the time we'd shared and everything he looked forward to, then gave me his best smile and pulled out a ring. Under other circumstances, I might've been swept off my feet, but I still had all of George's garbage clogging up my heart. I took several deep breaths, during which I saw his smile fall, then finally told him I'd have to think about it. He closed his mouth, nodded, put the ring away, and we finished dinner.

That night, while I was running John's proposal through my head over and over, George gave me another call. I don't remember what either of us said, but I do remember that in a state of panic, I did the unthinkable: I agreed to give him another chance.

John called the next morning, asking if we could get together and talk things out. I told him about George. There was a long silence over the line, until John finally told me, "I understand, but it won't work, and I'm going to wait. I'll wait for you." I thanked him for his understanding, then hung up, wondering what the hell I'd gotten myself into.

George started things off by doing everything he could to make up for all the bad times. He upgraded my wedding ring to a three-karat diamond ring, surprised me one day with a brand new Coupe de Ville Cadillac (with a crisp white exterior and all-black plush leather interior, just the way he knew I liked it), and when I told him, "No more apartments," he listened and moved us into a house.

We lived with the children in Gardena, in a four-bedroom home at the end of a cul-de-sac. Along with the four bedrooms, it came with a large living room, backyard, and a two-car garage. It even came with a nice-sized family room, and I furnished it with the newest floor model color television and leather couches. On top of that, I added an indoor/outdoor playroom for the kids, where their bikes, toys and art supplies were stored.

Two months after we moved, we had our third child, Karen. Karen Denise Washington. She was a beautiful baby. She had the cutest little dimples and a head full of hair. Karen made our little family complete.

Upgrading and beautifying our house became my new passion. All of the furniture came from Sloan's in Beverly Hills. I had expensive and good taste. Before long, we had Karastan Blue wool wall-to-wall carpet and ceiling to floor curtains in almost every room – the best money can buy. The living room had a blue and green silk custom-made couch. Green satin and orange tufted chairs complemented an extra thick glass coffee table, with bases made of gold lion statues. Our bedroom furniture was custom made as well, to our exact taste, with a dark headboard and a white custom made bedspread with gold trim. It looked like a bridal suite, complete with a real fireplace. The size of our home couldn't have been more perfect for our growing family. Valerie, our oldest, had a pink and white bedroom, while Gregory and Karen shared a blue and white room. The children took private swimming, tennis, and ballet lessons.

I lived like a Hollywood starlet without the fame. Along with the new house came more extravagant amenities, like diamond jewelry, mink coats, and a private masseuse who came to the house once a week for private massages.

George was also spending more time with us as a family. We took trips to Disneyland and started a weekly tradition of going to a popular Chinese Restaurant in Chinatown. Finally, we'd worked out all the flaws in our relationship and started living the life we were always meant to have – or so I thought.

It wasn't long before George started to show his true colors again. My gut always knew he would, and I could never shake my suspicions about all the material pleasures being a cover for his old habits, but I held out the hope that he'd changed. Unfortunately, if anything, he'd changed for the worse.

I saw the first sign as soon as I returned home from delivering Karen. As I carried her to the bedroom for the first time, I couldn't help but notice suspicious mustard stains on one of the rugs in the hallway. Someone had attempted to remove the stains, and had only made it worse. Before long, George's "late nights at the office" started getting later and later again, and the same with his "weekend work." One night, I remember sitting in the kitchen after midnight, when George finally walked through the door. There was no way he'd been working that late, and I knew it.

He closed the door, then turned around and did a double take when he saw me marching toward him. "Why are you up so late?" he asked.

I didn't respond; I just swung my fist at him hard as I could. George ducked, and I hit the door behind him, almost breaking my hand.

He tried to wave me off. "You need to stop that. You are going to hurt yourself. It's so unnecessary."

"'Unnecessary'? You're lucky I don't shoot your head off."

George shook his head. "You're crazy. You know that?"

"If I'm crazy, then you made me this way."

I took a long, hard look at the man I'd devoted my life to. All I could see was ugly. I knew then and there that he was never going to change, not for me, not for his kids, not for anybody. All I could do was come to terms with that.

That year, George left for "work" the day before Christmas, and didn't come back until the day after New Year's. My three children and I spent that Christmas without him. Karen was only 6 months old, but even she knew he was missing.

It was December 1963, and the radio was full of two things: Replays of Nat King Cole's Christmas song, and incessant reminders of the country crumbling all around me. President Kennedy had been shot and killed just a month before.

When George finally came back, in 1964, all he did was stroll in, scoff at me, walk straight into the bedroom, and slam the door behind him. I fell back down into my kitchen chair. I could feel my heart racing.

I went to see Dr. Jones again. Near the end of our hour, she looked at me and said, "Betty, what do want to do for yourself that you haven't already done?"

I stared at Dr. Jones, trying to gather up an answer to her question. Then it hit me: "I never finished my education at Howard University. Instead, I worked years as a clerk typist to put George through dental school."

Dr. Jones smiled, put down her pen and said, "Well, don't you think you should finish that?"

I nodded. "Yes, that's exactly what I'll do."

The next month, I enrolled in Pepperdine University to major in psychology with a minor in sociology. I was so determined to obtain my degree that one time, when a babysitter wasn't available, I took Gregory and Karen with me to my music class. The professor asked about a simple melody, showing us different arrangements. The song was Three Blind Mice. The professor asked if anyone in the class recognized the song.

My son Gregory blurted out, "I do!"

The entire class roared with laughter.

Having kids wasn't all that singled me out at Pepperdine. I was constantly aware that I was an adult in my 30s, and that almost all the other students were much younger. Most of the student body was white, with very few blacks. There were a few African students – even one pigmy – but we were part of a very small minority. Pepperdine was a very Protestant school, which meant we were all required to go to chapel at noon every day. We sang hymns and heard a scriptural reading. It didn't matter what your faith was; chapel attendance was mandatory, and if you didn't like it, the university made it clear you could attend another school. It was a radical adjustment from my experience at Howard University, a historically black college.

I made acquaintances with a few women who were older than myself, in their 50's. We studied together sometimes, but I mostly went to school, did my work, and came directly home.

The more I engrossed myself in school, the more I completely detached from George. I stopped sleeping in the same bed with him. I only cooked for my children and myself. If there was an event I had to attend, I put on a front and went as the dutiful wife, but that was far as I went for him.

Things went from "that bad" to "even worse" when I discovered that George's New Jersey lover was suing him. I learned she came to visit him in

California several times, staying in our apartment when Gregory was born – and in our *home* when Karen was born. Just the thought of another woman in *my* house and *my* bed made me sick.

I wanted to kill him.

I didn't. I held on somehow, for myself and my children, day after day.

George walked around with her lawsuit's legal papers in his jacket for almost a week straight, leaving his jacket open, clearly allowing me to see them. I wasn't sure if he was just stupid or actually wanted me to find them. Either way, his womanizing ways, along with his blatant disrespect, again threw me into deep sadness and self-loathing.

I finally took his flagrant indiscretion as an invitation to read the legal papers. As I flipped through the pages with my shaking hands, I learned the other woman was a RN, whom George had been seeing during his residency in New Jersey (while I was conveniently living with his in-laws in Maryland). The affair had apparently gone on for years, to the point where she'd loaned George money – to help support "his wife's fatal illness." To be fair, he'd used part of that money to pay for the birth of my first two children, but the rest had gone to himself and his practice.

I shook my head in disbelief. George had done many scandalous things in his life, but this was by far the worst. A creeping rage overtook every inch of me as I placed the papers down on the table and sat in silence.

It was over. I couldn't pretend any longer. Sleeping in separate beds didn't cut it anymore. I needed George out of my life once and for all.

I called my girlfriend Della and told her everything about the lawsuit. The first thing she told me to do was to make copies of all the papers. The second was to meet with her attorney. He advised me to close the joint accounts and open a major account in my name only, which I did. This time, I told myself, I would not turn back.

The attorney then gave me quitclaim documents to remove George's name from the property. I asked why, and he explained that in the event of a lawsuit against George, no one would be able to take the house from me or my children.

The night I presented all of this to George, his face went blank. He then uttered in a soft, defeated voice, "Now the house is all yours."

Even in defeat, he looked like scum. I didn't even bother following him to his gatherings anymore; no point in keeping up the front. Despite the progress I'd made, I slid further into a slump, making it even more difficult to just get out of the bed in the morning. The few people who saw me could tell right away how miserable I was; I'd given years to this man, been a fool the whole time, and now, aside from the children, nothing else mattered.

Well, not quite "nothing." You see, I should have mentioned this earlier, but by this point, I'd been seeing someone else too.

A Coupe de Ville Cadillac. One of my prized possessions. Mine looked just like this one.

Me, aka "Betty Bang Bang," in my new home in Gardena, California.

Gregory, Karen (in baby seat) and Valerie at home.

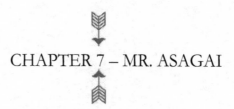

CHAPTER 7 – MR. ASAGAI

Let me turn things back a year or two, to 1963.

One Friday night, my good friend Adelaide called me and invited me to the movies. "Betty," she said, "They're showing *A Raisin in the Sun* at the theater. Have you seen it? I missed it the first time. It's got Sidney Poitier, Ruby Dee, *and* Diana Sands!" The excitement in her voice was hard to miss. This was back before home video, and with only three major TV networks, you either saw a picture when it first came out in the theater, or you usually didn't see it at all. Getting to see one you missed before was a rare opportunity.

"That sounds fun, Adelaide. Why don't I pick you up at 6:30 for the showing at 7:00?"

That night, my life took a drastic turn. The most incredible thing happened to me at that 7:00 pm showing. I still remember that moment when the actor playing the African student, Mr. Asagai, came through the door and smiled at the college student played by Diana Sands. I flipped inside. He only had one other scene, near the end of the movie, and I don't remember anything else about the movie at all. But I do remember every frame of his time onscreen.

I'd never believed in love at first sight, but the moment I saw him, my perception changed for good. Everything I'd known up until that point became a blur, replaced with a newfound bliss. Yes, I was in love, with a man I'd never met: An actor named Ivan Dixon.

*****

I can still remember the rush of sensations I felt as Adelaide and I left the theater that night. It was as if I had taken my first sip of water after living in the desert and drinking sand for years. I was in love – with a man I had only laid eyes on for minutes, but that was all it took to know how I felt.

"Are you all right?" Adelaide asked with a laugh when she noticed my breathing.

"I'm in love with the guy who played the African Student," I said.

"You mean Ivan Dixon?" Adelaide replied.

"Is that his name? Then yes, I'm in love with Ivan Dixon," I proclaimed. Funny; I hadn't even known his name, and I was already head over heels.

I drove Adelaide home, and when we parked on the street, we both got out. I turned to her, with conviction in my voice, and said, "I want to come in and use your telephone directory to see if Ivan lives in LA."

Adelaide laughed at me again. "Are you mad?"

"No, I'm not mad. I'm in love, and I need to find him."

Adelaide chuckled, probably thinking this was all a game I was playing.

"Seriously, Betty, you're not thinking. Say you get his number. What're you going to do with it?"

"I'm going to call him and say, 'I just saw you in *A Raisin in the Sun*, and I'm in love with you.'"

Adelaide shook her head. "He'll probably say, 'Great!' Then he'll hang up on you and think you're some crazy lady."

She had a point, but I stood my ground. Sighing, she crossed her arms and leaned against my white Coupe de Ville, "You can't be serious. Think about what you're about to do. You really can't do that."

As we headed for her front door, she continued to plead her case. "Seriously, Betty, you're not thinking this through."

By the time we reached her door, I started thinking she might have a point. Maybe calling up a total stranger and saying you're in love *was* crazy. I succumbed to my friend's logic. "Okay, you're right, Adelaide. I'll let it go."

As the next day went by, I caught myself thinking about Ivan more and more. Thinking that maybe I shouldn't have listened to Adelaide. The more I thought about Ivan, the less depressed I felt. That was a sure sign that I was in love. Occasionally, I would stop myself and chuckle at how I was carrying on, laughing at the idea of professing my love to a man who didn't even know I existed.

Yes, it was madness, but it felt good to be in love.

*****

A few months later, the Medical Dental Pharmaceutical Auxiliary was planning its first variety show. This was back when I was still keeping up the front with George, so that Saturday night, off we went together. I volunteered to pass out programs, since that was all the only talent I could muster up.

The evening was very entertaining, to say the least. My gynecologist played the violin. His physician friend, a cardiologist, played the part of a gangster, doing a one-man show. Halfway through his act, he forgot his lines, and brought down the house when he stood there by himself looking dazed and confused. My doctor could play the violin too, but made some squeaky notes as the audience howled with laughter.

When the curtains went down for intermission, I asked my friend Thelma to go to the powder room with me. Thelma and I walked through the theater, still tickled from the show's last few acts. For once, my spirits were high – and I had no idea how much higher they were about to get.

As we left the powder room, I froze and stared ahead, transfixed in disbelief. Standing no more than ten feet in front of me was the love of my life, Ivan Dixon himself.

I didn't move. I couldn't. I remember Thelma nudging me out of her way, but even then I stood stock still, my feet planted on the floor – at least, I assume they were planted there, since I couldn't even feel my legs. All I could do was stare at him, drowning in his presence while he chatted with two other actors.

"Move," Thelma commanded as she prodded me in the back. At that, Ivan turned to look in my direction. For just a moment, our eyes locked, and I think our hearts connected, as a big smile spread across his beautiful ebony smooth skin. His teeth sparkled and his eyes danced to the tune of my rapidly beating heart. Still in awe, I couldn't say a word.

Ivan broke my trance as he looked over his shoulder to make sure I was looking at him. There was no one behind him, so he had to have known it was me. He'd smiled at me. I don't even remember smiling back – just staring.

Then I heard a voice call my name. Not his voice. George's.

"Come on," he said. "You're going to miss the rest of the show."

If Ivan's stare had taken my breath away, George's voice shoved it back down my throat. Feeling started pouring back into my legs, like concrete. I walked right past Ivan. I didn't look at him again; I didn't have the nerve for it. But even as I fixed my eyes on the theater door, I felt his presence brush against mine, and I think he felt it too. Our bodies and souls passed each other like ships in the sea, shining lights at each other all the while.

I stepped back into the theater and took my assigned seat next to George. I don't even remember the second half of the show. Maybe it was fantastic; I don't know. I just remember feeling like I was all by myself in that theater. Just me and my thoughts about Ivan.

I rode home in silence. For days afterwards, I couldn't think of anything but Ivan. And then, somewhere along the line, I remembered: *He still doesn't even know your name.*

CHAPTER 8 – BIG LOVE

For the next year, whenever I sank to my lowest points, I thought of Ivan's smile. It helped, but I never thought I'd see that smile again, never thought anyone else would smile at me the way he did. I needed love. Not from George; I'd given up on that. But from someone. Even if it took an affair, I needed it – and after all George had put me through, I deserved it.

In the late spring of 1964, the second annual show for the Medical Dental Pharmaceutical Committee rolled around, to be held in the Wilshire Ebell Theater in Los Angeles. George and I went together again – one of the last times we'd do that – and I wound up in charge of passing out programs. As one guest after another took a program and moved along, I entertained the thought that Ivan might show up. Of course, I thought, that was just fantasy; what were the odds of him randomly showing up in front of me twice in a row?

I was so busy telling myself it couldn't happen that it took me a moment to recognize him.

Once again, there we were, less than five feet apart in that same theater, in front of the same powder room, almost exactly where we stood a year ago. And once again, my brain and my mouth both shut down, and all I could do was stare.

He smiled at me again, just as I'd remembered and imagined. He was always handsome, but especially so in his black tailored pants and crisp gold-colored shirt. I wanted to scream out, "I'm in love with you," loud enough for all to hear, but my lips refused to part. There he was, and I knew it would only be a moment before he walked on out of my life again—

"I know your name," he said.

I blinked. Had I heard him right?

"It wasn't easy to find you, Betty," he said. Oh, my God. "No one wanted to help me. But," he spread his hands, "I'm listed, I live in Pasadena, and I hope you will call me." He smiled waiting for me to respond.

If I was frozen before, I was petrified now. I had to say something. Anything. But instead, all I could do was turn around and walk. I didn't even know where I was headed until I wound up in my seat. And that's when it finally hit me: He just told me where to find him.

I couldn't sleep that night. I hope you will call me. I kept hearing that. Every negative thought I could imagine swirled through my head, telling me I wasn't worthy of this man, that it was too good to be true.

For three whole months, I believed that. I went through the motions day to day, dressing the kids, going to school, tiptoeing towards divorce, and sinking deeper and deeper into my own private hell. Finally, I decided I had to make a change, and I picked up the phone and dialed Ivan's number.

Ring.

What was I doing? Did I even have a chance at this?

Ring.

What if George found out? What would he do?

Halfway through the third ring, I nearly hung up and told myself to forget about this whole charade, but I didn't. I knew if I stopped there, I'd never have the nerve to try again.

"Hello?" His voice was just as strong and gentle as when he'd called my name. My heart started pounding.

"Hi," I said, practically speechless again. "This is Betty Washington."

"What took you so long to call me?"

The sound of his voice was starting to relax me. "I had to get up the nerve."

There was a long pause, then: "When can I see you?"

"Tomorrow night would be good for me," I replied, faster than even I expected.

"Where do you live?" Ivan asked.

I didn't usually give out my personal information, but with him, I found I didn't mind at all. "I live in Gardena, not far from Compton. We could meet halfway, in LA." My breathing quickened. I couldn't believe this was happening.

Where could we go? I had to think fast. "I have a friend who lives near Crenshaw, off Santa Barbara," I said. "Let me call her right now, and ask if we can meet at her place." I took a deep breath. "Can I call you back in ten minutes?"

"Sure thing," Ivan responded before we both hung up.

I picked the phone back to call my friend Virginia. My hands were shaking, and I think my voice was too. "Virginia, I need a favor"

"What type of favor?" she asked.

"I need to meet a new friend at your apartment tomorrow. I need to leave my car and ride with him in his car."

Virginia let out a laugh and a squeal. "Finally! Better late than never, right? What's his name?"

I felt like a schoolgirl talking about her innocent crush. "Ivan Dixon."

I heard her gasp. "Ivan Dixon, the actor?"

"Yes, the actor. Virginia, I just need to park my car at your house. It won't be a visit."

Virginia laughed again. "Woman, you sure picked a hunk."

*****

I couldn't sleep a wink that night. All I could think about was my date tomorrow with the man I loved. My thoughts sank back to grade school, when dark-skinned boys used to snub me. George wasn't dark; he was high yellow, very tall, had gray-hazel eyes, and had hair that resembled a white boy's.

Ivan was dark and handsome, like my father. I wondered if the resemblance is what made me fall in love with him.

I continued to toss and turn. My excitement quickly turned to doubt, which quickly turned to frustration. What was I getting myself into? After about three hours of inner debate and external turmoil, I made the decision to just forget about everything and go with the flow. I took a deep breath, closed my eyes, and envisioned Ivan's beautiful face looking at me with that sparkle in his eye. I was in love with him, and that was all that mattered at the moment.

I don't remember any of the next day until about 7:00. By then, I was on the Harbor Freeway headed towards Los Angeles. I was shaking all over, partly from the anticipation and partly because I don't think I'd eaten all day. I flipped on the local jazz station to calm my nerves, and found the tantalizing sounds of Dizzy Gillespie. He was blowing on his horn something beautiful. Faster than I normally drive, I exited at Santa Barbara and headed down Crenshaw towards Virginia's apartment. I found a parking space just a few cars down from her place, quickly got out, and headed for her door.

Virginia buzzed me in before I even had a chance to ring the bell. She opened the door, her grin wide enough to fit a nice-sized hanger.

"Virginia, you need to check who's buzzing your bell before opening your door."

She laughed. "Woman, I saw you getting out of your car."

Virginia seemed even more excited than I was. She quickly closed the door behind me, then started throwing questions my way before I'd had a chance to cool my heels.

"So how on earth did you meet Ivan Dixon?"

A quick glance at my watch – 7:55 pm – told me I didn't have much time, so I gave Virginia the short version. By the end of it, her mouth was wide-open, still with a great big smile. She sat down, eyes open wide. "So this is your first date?"

I could see her gearing up to get a bit more personal than I was ready to share. Luckily for me, I looked out of her kitchen window to see Ivan pulling up behind my car. Thank God for small favors. I grabbed my purse and headed for her door.

"Well, there he is. I have to leave. Ivan's parking behind my car."

I was halfway out the door when I heard Virginia coming up behind me. "Wait a minute," she said. "I'm going to his car with you. I need to check his license plate."

Before she had a chance to put one foot outside, I put out a hand and stopped her. "Virginia, you have his name. He's not Jack the Ripper."

With that, I told her I'd call her later and closed the door behind myself.

Just before I stepped into Ivan's line of sight, I stopped and took a long, deep breath. "You can do this, Betty. He doesn't know how much you love him. That's your little secret."

Ivan saw me approaching his car, smiled, and immediately opened the door on my side. "Hello," he said, "how are you?"

I'd never felt so many butterflies flitting around in my stomach, but I still managed to look right into his eyes. "Okay," I said, taking a breath. "I'm okay."

I waved goodbye to Virginia, who was peering out her window like the neighborhood snoop, still grinning from ear to ear. Then I climbed into Ivan's car. He hurried to his side and slid in next to me. Outwardly, he seemed just as excited as I was. Inwardly, I'm sure I was twice as excited, but I made it a point to keep that from showing.

"So where would you like to go?" Ivan asked.

"I like the Malibu area. In fact, I really enjoy a couple of the Malibu restaurants on the coast," I said with a smile.

"Great, I know the perfect place," Ivan said as he flipped on the radio. A jazz station came on, and a melody of mixed instruments filled the car. Ivan turned back to me. "Do you like jazz, Betty?"

I smiled. This couldn't have been a more perfect start to a perfect first date.

"No, I love jazz. Matter of fact, my Auntie is Wee Bea Booze..."

"...the See See Rider Blues Girl," Ivan said, completing my sentence. "Impressive."

Ivan took on a calm, easy smile as he started up his car and slowly drove off. We headed down Crenshaw, onto the 10-West freeway, near the point where it drops down onto the Pacific Coast Highway. It was a beautiful evening, and as the setting sun kissed the ocean, Ivan and I soaked in the scene. We drove in silence all the way to Malibu.

Once we pulled up to the restaurant, Ivan quickly jumped out of the car and opened my door. "Shall we?" he asked, slowly reaching out for my hand. I gently slid mine into his.

His hands were soft as silk. He smoothly squeezed my hand, making sure I didn't let go. I was dancing inside as we slowly walked toward the door.

We were seated at a table facing the ocean. The night lay gently upon us. The air was getting cool, and the stars were bright. We had an amazing seat, with plush cushions and a sweeping view of the Pacific Ocean. Ivan sat close to me. I could feel his energy. My body tingled all over as we glanced each other's way like young kids in love.

The waiter came to take our order. Ivan turned to me to ask me what I drank.

"I would like vodka, orange juice, with lots of ice." I said.

Ivan looked at the waiter and ordered the same, one with lots of ice, one with easy ice.

We sat quietly for most of the night, listening to jazz. I didn't attempt to talk, nor did Ivan; we were simply enjoying each other's presence, and that was enough for the moment. Off to one side, a patron continued to feed a high-end-looking jukebox with coin after coin, and Sarah Vaughn filled the air with her sensual voice.

We sat close, the ocean waves dancing in a rhythmic pattern, crashing against the rocks below us. Ivan ordered a second round of drinks before he finally broke the silence. He slowly grabbed my hand and softly kissed it. I felt a tingle swirl through my skin.

Ivan's eyes moved up my body, toward my face, until our eyes locked. We were lost in a moment together, and then he punctuated it with one of the greatest things I'd ever heard:

"So, what are we going to do about this big love?"

I turned, slowly looking at him, but remaining silent. Ivan moved even closer to me, until finally, we kissed. It was a light, passionate kiss, and in that moment, our souls merged into one. The music stopped, everyone disappeared, and in our hearts and minds, we were the only two people to exist.

Then an image flashed into my head, etching its way into my memory as if it had always belonged. I saw myself and Ivan on the edge of a seaside cliff beneath a gorgeous sunset. He wore a black tux, with me in a beautiful ball gown the color of the sunset sky. We danced there together, brushing the edge with our feet, kicking sand down toward all the huge, sharp rocks in the surf below. I didn't even look at them. I knew, as long as I was in his arms, I'd never fall.

After an eternity, our lips parted, leaving both of us at a loss of words. My body still tingled like a fever in a wind.

"Are you okay, Bette?" Bette. No one had ever called me that.

"I'm good, just fine," I said, taking a deep breath and trying to regain my composure.

"Are you ready to go?"

"Yes…if you are?"

Ivan smiled and paid our tab. We left the restaurant and headed back down the Pacific Coast Highway towards LA. I glanced at Ivan a few times out of the corner of my eye. He had what looked like a permanent smile on his face. We rode in silence once again as jazz wafted gently from the radio. The route back to my car seemed unfamiliar, but I wasn't thinking just then. I was being.

Ivan turned down Olympic Boulevard from Santa Monica. I knew at that point I was not going back to my car, at least not anytime soon. Ivan turned into the Olympic Motor Inn. He parked in front of it, paused, then looked at me and said, "Sit tight. I'll be right back."

I nodded.

As I waited for Ivan to return, I took in my surroundings. I watched a young white couple pull up across from me. They got out and headed for the motel office. I wondered what their story was, wondered if they were in love like I was in love. Wondered if their life was about to change like I felt mine was about to. The couple disappeared behind the tinted glass door.

Ivan soon returned with the motel keys. He came around and opened my door. Together, we walked into the motel room.

The room was dimly lit and smelled of sweet lavender and lilacs. This definitely wasn't a five-star accommodation, but it was clean and cozy. It would do. There was a king-sized bed, two nightstands with mismatched lamps, a radio on one of those nightstands, and a small TV centered on a long oak dresser in front of the bed.

The floral bedspread matched the drapes perfectly, as if cut from the same roll, and I noticed that they were half open. Even though we were on the second floor, I didn't want to take any chances with a peeping Tom, so I walked over to the drapes and closed them.

Ivan turned on the radio. I just stood there and watched him. I had plenty of chances to say no, could have said, "I'm married," or "I'm not ready," but I didn't say a word. I let him move flawlessly toward me until we stood face to face. The soft scents of his cologne intoxicated me. I breathed him in deeply as we touched. I was warm, tingling, breathing heavily, but most of all, I was completely comfortable.

Ivan slowly began to undress me. I wore a white silk dress, with buttons all the way to the hem. We both kind of chuckled as a few buttons gave him a problem. He was careful not to tear them off, although at that point, I wouldn't have cared. Next he removed my bra, leaving nothing but my pantyhose.

Ivan scanned my body from head to toe as if he were inspecting a priceless piece of art. A new kind of smile raced across his face. I looked away, feeling just a bit uncomfortable about being examined. I was overweight, and not confident at all about my body. Ivan clearly felt differently; he dropped his hands, shook his head, and said in the sweetest voice ever, "You are so beautiful, Betty." His voice worked its magic and put me at ease. Ivan then undressed himself. He took off his pants and followed with his shirt. We stood in front of each other in nothing but underwear. He took another step closer, and we embraced, our bare chests touching.

We wrapped our arms around each other as if we were one, and felt the warmth between our bodies. Ivan leaned in. We kissed once again. His soft lips explored every part of my mouth. The warm sureness of Ivan's kiss, and his gentle, large hands around my bare waist, sent chills down my spine, chills I'd never felt before. Ivan continued to kiss me with such care and passion that, for a moment, I forgot where I was; I was losing myself in his touch, his kiss, his soul.

We slowly made our way to the bed. Ivan laid me down and gently lay beside me. We said nothing, for no words were needed; it was as if we could read each other's minds. Our union was bliss. Our bodies moved in unison as we embraced each other tightly, staying in the moment until the very end.

After our breathless lovemaking, I don't know what came over me. I jumped out of the bed and ran into the bathroom. I definitely surprised Ivan, as he sat up in bed, leaned against the headboard, and craned his neck over curiously.

I came back into the bedroom, dressed in a large white towel. Then I gave Ivan a broad, seductive smile as I moved over to the radio and flipped the dial until I heard Aretha Franklin singing "Respect." The beat guided me into a solo bump and grind, giving Ivan a private dance. I was on another planet, a world of unconditional love and respect.

Ivan just watched with a big grin on his face as his head bopped to the music. He began to laugh. "Bette, you are light on your feet," he told me as he continued to groove to the beat.

I finished my dance and leaped into Ivan's arms with a laugh. "I love to dance," I told him. I felt so safe in that moment, as if I could tell Ivan anything and everything. I think he felt the same way, because we spent the rest of the night getting to know each other better.

Of course, it wasn't all fun and romance; I was expecting the inevitable crashing back to Earth when he would tell me this was a one-time thing. I didn't have to wait long for the other shoe to drop.

Ivan looked at me with his vibrant brown eyes, "Bette." He looked down, then back up. His voice softened. "There's something I should have told you…"

Oh, God, I thought, this can't be good…

He went on, "I'm telling you now because I want you in my life, and you deserve to know the truth." He took a long pause, and I almost wondered if he'd decided not to tell me anything. Then, finally: "I'm married."

I recoiled. Why hadn't I thought of that? Why did I think everything was going to be perfect? I didn't know what to think…but, I realized, I only needed a moment to know what to feel. I stopped, took a deep breath, let my heart speak its piece, and I knew then and there that my feelings for him hadn't changed.

"I have two sons," he said, staring at the floor again and shaking his head. "Wonderful boys…"

"I have two girls and one son," I told him. At that, he looked up at me again, and he dared to smile.

We sat there together quietly. He reached out and stroked my face, "You are so very beautiful," he said. "Young face for a mother of three. How old are you?"

"Thirty-four," I answered very quickly.

Ivan's eyebrows jumped, "I'd have thought you were younger." Another long silence passed as he went on brushing his fingers against my cheek. I could almost see his words gathering until he finally asked, "So, your children. Is their father all right?"

"He…" I gave Ivan a very serious look, to the point where he lowered his fingers. "We don't have a relationship. We don't love each other anymore. We live a lie."

As I spoke, Ivan placed his hand over mine. His touch radiated love and support. I continued, "We put on a front for his friends, we show up together at his big events, but we don't even share the same bed."

Ivan didn't say anything; he just continued to caress my hand, looking deep into my eyes. I didn't feel the urge to ask him anything personal; maybe I just didn't want to know. Maybe I felt like the less I knew about him and his life, the less it would affect my feelings for him – especially since I was so in love.

After finally leaving the hotel and heading back to retrieve our cars, we talked all the way to our destination.

"Bette, are you free next Monday for lunch? You can come down to the studio, and I can show you around," Ivan said minutes after we pulled away from the motel.

"Yes, that would be lovely."

"When's the best time to call you?"

"Anytime you like," I said.

Ivan looked a bit surprised with my answer, but it was the truth. I was available for his call at any time of the day.

We finally pulled up to my car. Ivan jumped out and opened my door. I felt like he'd catered to me all night, and I didn't want it to end. I stepped out of the car, and Ivan closed the door behind me, planting a soft goodbye kiss on my cheek. "I had a great time with you tonight, Bette."

"I had a wonderful time with you, Ivan."

We smiled like two lovesick teenagers.

"I'm going to follow you home to make sure you get there safely. Is that okay?"

"Yes, and thank you," I said as I headed to my car and started my engine. I pulled out of the parking spot, and there was Ivan right behind me. He indeed followed me all the way home that night. It was late, and I was glad he was such a gentleman to do that.

I drove home with the radio on, setting a soundtrack to the thoughts that danced in my head. If I never saw Ivan again, I would never forget our night and our undeniable connection. I'd always known, from the first time I laid eyes on Ivan, that he was my soulmate for life, and now I was beyond sure of it.

Ivan Dixon, the love of my life.

CHAPTER 9 – DESILU

My date with Ivan pulled me out of my decline. So much so that even my eldest daughter, Valerie, noticed my mood swing. One day, Valerie said to me, "Mommy, you are happy." Then, "So I'm happy because you're happy."

I gave my daughter a big hug. "Thank you, Valerie, I am very happy."

Every day was like a new day for me. I was seeing things much more clearly, and my spirit was singing a song of joy and happiness.

I made the decision to not put any pressure on Ivan. I would see him when he was available, expect nothing, and make no demands.

A few days after Ivan and I spent that glorious night together in Malibu, he called for the first time. It was a beautiful Sunday afternoon, and hearing his voice made my heart sing.

"Bette, I wanted to give you directions to Desilu Studios on Gower. That's where I'm shooting this new show, called *Hogan's Heroes*."

I quickly grabbed a pen and paper and jotted down every detail of his directions.

"You got everything?" he asked.

"Yes. I'll see you tomorrow," I said, hoping I wasn't being too obvious with my excitement.

"Great, I can't wait to see you, Bette," Ivan said, and he hung up the phone.

Although it was just a day away, I wanted to see him *now*. I kept envisioning his tender touch and our sensual kisses. Just thinking about it sent those butterflies flitting inside me all over again.

Monday finally came, and I asked my new nanny Dada to stay a few extra hours to baby-sit. Dada, a heavyset woman with salt and pepper hair, happily agreed, shooting me one of her legendary smiles that could warm the sun.

I arrived on the set around noon. Ivan had arranged for me to park in the studio parking lot, so I wouldn't have to walk too far. I greeted the security guard with a smile. He pulled out Ivan's guest list and tapped my name, and just that gesture warmed me up inside. After the security guard checked my ID and let me pass, I cruised through Desilu Studios as if I were important.

I later found out that Desilu Studios' name came from its two owners, Desi Arnaz and Lucille Ball. The studio was home to legendary TV shows like *I Love Lucy, The Untouchables,* and the original *Star Trek.*

I drove between two sound stages, massive cream-colored buildings at least ten stories high. After finally finding a place to park, I got out of my car, smoothing my white ruffled shirt and navy blue skirt. It was a hot day, and I enjoyed the warm sun as it beamed down on my skin.

I followed Ivan's directions toward his trailer. On the way, I passed another trailer, where *My Three Sons* star Fred MacMurray was sitting under a blue awning, puffing away on a cigar. I glanced at him, sitting outside with a jacket around his back. He looked up at me and smiled. I returned his smile and kept walking. He seemed relieved that I didn't stop to ask him for his autograph. I would have been too busy to ask him if I'd wanted to, but I wasn't some giddy fan anyway. I liked to think that I respected acting, and those who pursued it as a profession.

I finally found Ivan's trailer and lightly knocked. Ivan opened the door, a broad smile running across his face.

"Hello there," he said. "I'm glad you could make it. Are you hungry?"

"Yes, a bit," I replied.

"Let me get my jacket and we can grab something," Ivan said as he headed back into his trailer. The blue sports jacket completed his casual outfit, with khaki pants on a crisp white shirt. I assumed that was his attire for the shoot that day. Of course, he looked good in anything.

I was so busy taking in the sight of him that I nearly forgot the present I'd brought. Reaching into a bag, I pulled out a copy of a book called *Social Problems*. I'd had it with me earlier, since I'd recently changed my major from psych to sociology with a minor in psych, and he'd asked me for a loaner copy so that he could keep up with what I was reading. I liked that about him; he not only wanted to be my lover, but my intellectual partner too. He accepted the book with a grin, then headed out with me.

We ended up going to the commissary. The food there was surprisingly good. I had grilled chicken with asparagus, and Ivan had fish with mashed potatoes. Our lunch was quick, since I had to head back to avoid freeway traffic. I'd have stuck around regardless, traffic being a small price to pay for Ivan's company, but he didn't want me bogged down in rush hour. His gentlemanly ways were very refreshing, and they always made me smile.

"Thank you for coming all the way down here," Ivan said to me as we headed back towards my car.

"No problem," I said. "Thank you for calling."

He stopped and turned toward me. "Bette, what are you doing this weekend?"

Even if I'd had plans, I'd have canceled them. "Nothing I can recall at the moment."

"Great. Well, tell me then, which night's best for you, Friday or Saturday?

"Saturday," I replied.

"Perfect. We'll go to listen to jazz at the Lighthouse in Redondo Beach." Ivan said, opening my car door for me. I slid behind the seat of my white Cadillac.

"That sounds good," I said.

I loved that Ivan took charge, and I didn't mind at all. The more I got to know him, the more I saw how much we had in common.

We arrived at the Lighthouse jazz club that Saturday around 8pm. They sat us down near the front, which had a perfect view of both the beach and the music. Ivan ordered drinks for us, and we spent the evening immersed in the tunes of a modern jazz quartet.

During intermission, several actors from Ivan's TV series came into the club too. For the first time, it hit me: We were acting like two married people out together. It was okay when Ivan and I were alone, but meeting people and being introduced to his friends made me uneasy. I saw them heading our way, and I immediately went to the powder room.

I stood in the mirror, staring into my reflection. I tried to shake off my doubts and my guilt – especially my guilt; what did I owe George? – but I couldn't. I thought about leaving and explaining to Ivan later, but I ended up staying so long in the powder room that Ivan sent the waitress to check on me. I told her nicely that I would be out in a minute.

One minute turned into 15, and the next thing I knew, Ivan was walking through the door of the ladies' powder room. I looked up at him, and he immediately reached for my hand. As soon as we touched, all my doubts evaporated.

"Bette, these guys are friends of mine. They're not going to sit at our table. I'll just give you a quick introduction, and you don't even have to say a thing, okay?"

I nodded and he led me back to our table.

We took our seats, and I met all his actor friends one by one. One of the actors was Greg Morris, a handsome black actor about my age. I hadn't heard much about him at the time, but he'd go on to appear in many roles throughout the 60's, 70's, and 80's, including his best-known role on the *Mission Impossible* series. His body of work made him a big star in "Black Hollywood," and he paved the way for many black actors today. He and Ivan's other friends were all very polite as we shook hands and said our hellos.

After they left, Ivan turned to me and smiled. "Now, that wasn't so bad, was it?"

I returned Ivan's smile, "Well, I guess it wasn't *so* bad." Nice as his friends were, the fact remained that I was a married woman out with a married man.

My conscience was starting to gnaw at me, but I quickly shooed it aside. My love for Ivan had a way of justifying my actions. I'd already decided I would continue to see Ivan as long as he made me feel like this. I didn't want to lose what we had, and definitely didn't want to lose the feeling that rose inside me every time he looked my way. I wanted to wrap that feeling around my heart and keep it there forever.

CHAPTER 10 – I'M NOT GOING TO HIDE YOU

Time started passing very quickly. It had been 2 months already since our first date. Ivan was great at keeping in contact with me and making time to fit me into his schedule.

He would even ask about my children, Gregory in particular. In fact, we talked about our families often. I would never say anything disparaging to Ivan about his wife; it wasn't my place, and I never wanted to be disrespectful. He and I were becoming close, very close.

Every one of our dates was a new adventure. He took me to places and restaurants I never could have hoped to experience. He opened my world up in ways George had always tried to close down.

I never called it "love." Not openly, and not while he was in earshot. But I think Ivan knew I was in love with him. And, being so wrapped up in my own feelings, I didn't think to wonder at the time if he might be in love with me. Was he? He didn't say the words, but the warmth between us told me he'd never need to.

One afternoon, Ivan and I were having lunch at a Yamashiro's, a classy Japanese restaurant high above Hollywood Boulevard. He looked at me and plainly said, "Bette, I want you to meet my best friend."

I smiled and just said, "Okay."

"Okay," Ivan echoed with much enthusiasm. We finished lunch in a hurry, then jumped in his car and headed down Sunset to Mulholland Drive. I could tell this was a special occasion for him, which made me wonder who this person could possibly be.

As we got closer to his house, I turned to Ivan and asked him, "Who's your friend?"

Ivan glanced over at me and replied, "Sidney Poitier."

My stomach did a weird turn. We'd talked about this before; I wanted to spend what little free time I had with him. It may have been wrong, but I didn't care about meeting his friends or being in Hollywood. "Ivan, would you mind if I just stayed in the car?" I said, hoping I didn't sound too upset.

Ivan frowned and did a double take. "Why? I told him I was bringing you to meet him."

I was quiet. I didn't want to hurt Ivan's feelings. Meeting his friend had nothing to do with him; it had everything to do with me just wanting to be with Ivan, period. But when I saw the disappointment in Ivan's eyes, I knew that meeting Sidney would mean the world to him.

"Okay, I'll meet your friend."

We drove up the driveway to a beautiful home. The view was magnificent. Overwhelmingly so. I wondered how I could meet this man if his house alone was throwing me for such a loop.

As it turned out, the house wasn't his. When Ivan opened my door, he told me that this was Billy Daniels' house, and that Sidney was staying there for a while. I walked with Ivan to the front door, admiring the landscaping along the way. The combined aroma of the flowers tickled my nose with pleasure. Someone could have sold postcards of the place; it looked so bright and picture perfect.

When the door swung open, I was expecting a butler or housekeeper, but no, it was Sidney Poitier himself. He was wearing tan khaki pants with a white top, looking very comfortable and relaxed. He was taller than I'd imagined, and his skin was silky smooth and clean as spring water rain. Ivan and Sidney greeted each other with a warm hug.

Ivan turned to me and extended his hand. Making no attempt to hide his excitement, he said, "Sid, this is Bette. Bette, this is Sid."

I stretched out my hand, and as our hands connected, we both said our hellos.

Ivan and I entered the beautifully decorated home. I swept my eyes over the walls, floor, and ceiling in awe. We entered the living room, where one entire wall was fully mirrored. While the room was very large to begin with, the mirrors mounted on the wall made it look twice as big. There was a very plush sofa and chairs, just as plush, with a very thick white carpet.

I imagined Ivan and myself living together in a home like this, happy and carefree. I smiled at the thought.

Ivan and Sidney chatted. You could tell they were very good friends trying to catch up as men do. Ivan kept trying to include me into the conversation, but it was no use; I had nothing to contribute to their stories. I just sat in silence and watched Ivan enjoy his friend's company.

During their visit, a phone rang relentlessly. A heavyset maid, who looked to be in her 50's, opened the door and said, "Mr. Poitier, this call is very urgent."

Sidney acknowledged her request, excused himself, and left the room. Once he was gone, Ivan turned to me with a sudden scowl. "Bette," he said, "why are you being so unfriendly? Sid is going to think you don't like him."

For the first time in our relationship, I snapped back at Ivan. "Like him? I don't even know him. He's your friend, not mine." I felt my heart speed up with each word that escaped my lips.

Ivan saw my irritation and quickly changed the subject. "Do me a favor, will you? Sid wants to learn that dance, 'the Jerk.' I told him you were light on your feet. Will you please teach him to do the Jerk?" A soft smile crept across his face.

I couldn't stay mad at Ivan, not for one minute. Before I even had a chance to answer, Sidney was walking back into the living room. Ivan turned to Sid and said, "Sid, Bette is going to teach you to do the Jerk."

Sidney looked and kind of laughed. He was probably a little embarrassed that Ivan had made it known he couldn't dance.

"We need some music," I injected. "With a beat," I quickly added. The Jerk requires a two-step beat, and I wanted to make sure Sidney put on the right kind of music.

"Music with a beat, coming right up," Sidney confirmed. He walked over to the radio sitting on the mahogany bookshelf and turned it on. He flipped through the stations until he heard one with a fast enough tempo. Marvin Gaye's voice filled the room. Sidney turned to me to see if I approved of the song selection.

"Perfect," I said as I moved to the mirror. I motioned for Sidney to get on my left side. We looked at ourselves in the mirror as I started Jerking. Sidney just stood there, stiff as a board, but studying my every move. I guess that's what actors do; they study their subjects first before attempting to copy them.

I continued to dance and watched him studying me. "Sidney, move your body and try to slowly follow what I'm doing."

A sheepish smile spread over Sidney's face as he began to emulate me. I have to say, his version of the Jerk looked a whole lot different than mine.

We both laughed in good fun. Despite my best efforts, I couldn't teach Sidney to Jerk that day, but all and all, it was a good day regardless.

Later that night, Ivan and I ended up at the Chateau Marmont on Sunset Boulevard for drinks and jazz. The Chateau was modeled after an infamous royal residence in France's Loire Valley, a fantastical folly in the land of make believe. Its eccentric history charmed me instantly with its rich luscious past and exquisite charm. Ivan and I would end up going there frequently.

I loved the way the place made me feel. Surrounded by the personal history of people like Howard Hughes and Greta Garbo, I would sink into one of the deep couches and let the smoky jazz fill my ears. Sidney had an apartment at the Chateau. Ivan had the keys, and we would often meet there for drinks.

One night at our usual spot, the Olympic Motor Inn, I got a tremendous surprise. Ivan and I had just finishing making love, and I had decided to take a shower. As I was lathering my entire body from head to toe, Ivan opened the door and stepped inside the shower with me. He looked at me and just smiled, then slowly started washing my back. I couldn't speak.

I felt a sweet sensation trickle down my spine as Ivan cleansed my entire back from my shoulders down. I had never taken a shower with my husband; this was a first for me, one of the many firsts I experienced with Ivan. He was taking me places emotionally I never thought I could go. Not with George, and not with anyone else but Ivan.

After washing my back, he stepped out of the shower and stood there. The water washed all over me, getting my hair wet. In that moment, I decided to cut my hair and go all-natural. I admired a South African Singer by the name of Miriam Makeba; that was how I would cut my hair, exactly like hers.

I ended up going to Ivan's barber to get my Makeba Afro. He was located on Crenshaw Boulevard in Los Angeles.

"Please don't tell Ivan what I'm doing. I want it to be a surprise," I told the barber.

"He won't hear it from me," his barber assured me. I left the barbershop feeling like a new woman, and couldn't wait to show off my new hairdo.

About a week later, Ivan and I decided to meet at the Chateau. We were in the mist of deciding whether to go to jazz or a movie when the phone rang. I had on a wig, so Ivan wouldn't see my surprise haircut until I could show it to him my way.

Ivan took the call, and I quietly went into the bathroom to remove my wig. I had a moment of doubt – *What if he doesn't like it?* – but there was no going back now. I took a deep breath and stepped into the living room.

I walked back out just when he finished his call. As soon as he saw me, he sprang to his feet, yelling, "Oh my God, oh my God!"

He broke into a grin, rushed towards me, grabbed me, and twirled me around and around yelling, "Oh my God, I am not going to hide you. I am not going to hide you!"

Ivan kept repeating that same phrase over and over as he continued to twirl me around the room. At first, I didn't understand what he meant; I hadn't thought that we *were* hiding.

Then he put me down, looked at me, and said, "I know this beautiful place on Restaurant Row. It's got dancing, and *we are going dancing!*"

We went to the nicest restaurant on La Cienega; they even had live violin music. Ivan, deliriously happy, twirled me around the dance floor with a constant smile on his face.

Finally, the violinists took a break, and so did we. One of Ivan's friends approached our table, an actor named Yaphet Kotto. I wasn't very familiar with his work, but I made like I was. Kotto wouldn't stop staring at me, and at one point told Ivan, "This woman's face is a work of art."

Ivan beamed and said to him, "I know, yes she is."

I never said a word, but I think Ivan was getting used to my silence when I was around his friends.

We continued to enjoy our night together. I just loved being with Ivan; it was as if time stood still when we were in each other's world. We were just finishing up our second round of drinks when Ivan took my hand, held it tightly, and looked me deep in the eye.

"Bette," he said, "I need to ask George's permission to date you. I need George's phone number."

I could tell he wasn't joking, so I kept quiet as he went on to say, "I can't take any chances that will jeopardize my career. I've worked too hard to get to this point. I don't want a scandal. Actors are constantly in the spotlight. Black actors get *two* spotlights." He let me chuckle at that, then continued. "So the best thing for me to do is call your husband and ask for his permission to date you...publicly."

"Publicly?" I repeated.

"Bette, I'm not going to hide you. This has to be completely out in the open."

I sat for a few more seconds before tearing off a piece of a napkin and taking out a pen. I wrote down George's number and handed it to Ivan. He smiled, we had a couple more drinks, and then he stood, held out his hand, and walked me out.

As Ivan and I left the restaurant that night, I knew everything about my life – our lives – would change. For the better, I hoped, but all I could do was pray.

Me, after I cut my hair and went natural.

Another shot just after my haircut.

CHAPTER 11 – YOUR BOYFRIEND CALLED

It wasn't until several nights later when Ivan's intent made its way into reality. I was sitting in the living room, reading a schoolbook, when George came home earlier than usual. I was usually asleep by the time he came home, but not tonight. Tonight, he was home before I had a chance to take my nightly bath.

George walked through the open hall doorway. He began to remove his jacket, then followed that by yanking off his tie. He didn't say a word when he headed over to the liquor cabinet and started making a drink. While stirring his Jack Daniels on the rocks, he looked over at me.

"Your boyfriend called," he said. "He's asking for my permission to take you out. Hrmph."

George downed his drink and set his glass on the bar, "He said he was a 'prominent figure' and couldn't afford a scandal. He wanted to tell me his name but I said, 'I don't need to know your name.'" He slapped down a shotglass. "I told him, 'If *my* wife thinks *that* much of you to give you *my* phone number, then you have my permission.'." He poured a glass and a shot, then quaffed them both. "And then I hung up."

George replenished his drink and tossed the stirrer into the sink. I sat there, not moving a muscle, while he kept on staring at me. Finally, I decided I had nothing to say to him, and I just went back to my textbook.

He turned and stomped down the hallway until I heard the bedroom door slam. I smiled to myself, and felt a surge of elation dance throughout my body. Honestly, I was a little surprised that Ivan had actually called George, because he'd never told me when he was going to. But now the deed was done, and it felt good to have everything out in the open. George was finally getting a taste of his own medicine, and I couldn't have been happier. I was officially free to date Ivan.

And that wasn't the only big surprise that week. A day later, Ivan called me. When I picked up the phone, I heard Ivan, clear as a bell, say to me, "Bette, I need for you to meet my wife."

Well, I should have expected that at some point, but I hadn't. As soon as he said the words, my hand started shaking, so badly I thought I was going to drop the phone clear to the floor.

"Did you hear me, Bette?"

"Yes, I heard you," I answered.

Before I could ask why, Ivan was already explaining. "Our relationship has to be clear. It has to be out in the open, with no hiding and no mystery."

I was quiet, plotting my next words, slowly, carefully. I then asked, "When will

I meet her?"

"Let's meet tomorrow for lunch at the studio. I'll give you my address too. I don't live in Pasadena anymore; I live in Altadena."

"Okay, then. I'll see you tomorrow."

I hung up the phone, feeling a bit lightheaded. I asked myself how much I really understood about this man who had my heart. All I knew in that moment was that I loved him and would do anything to be with him – even meet his wife of ten years.

I arrived at Ivan's Altadena's home in the early evening. In the past, when I was going to meet Ivan, I would drive extremely fast to get there, but today, I found myself driving very slow – five miles under the speed limit.

It was a beautiful day, close to sunset, with a daze of light still shining down on his neighborhood. The yards were freshly manicured and flowers bloomed all over. Ivan's home was brand new.

He opened the door after my first ring. We stood staring at each other for a few seconds before he invited me into his home.

I followed Ivan inside. We walked through the tile-covered foyer and into the dining room, where his wife sat quietly in a high-back chestnut chair. She was gazing out the window as if she were studying something important, something she'd been trying to decipher for some time now.

Our entrance disturbed her solitude. She turned towards us and stared directly into my eyes. She didn't smile, get up or gesture; she just stared, studying and evaluating me. I was the woman her husband wanted her to meet, the woman he was spending his free time with. The woman who was now standing less than 10 feet away from her.

Her name was Berlie, and she was a very attractive light-skinned woman with a medium build. She wore a light shade of lipstick, and no other makeup from what I could gather. She wore her hair naturally, and dressed in African attire. She made me feel uninvited, though I could certainly understand why. Ivan sat me directly across from her as we continued to stare at each other. I wasn't sure who would turn away first, but I was determined it wouldn't be me.

Ivan stood at the head of the table, directly between us, like a boxing referee ready to begin Round One.

"Ladies, I have you two here for a reason," Ivan said as he rubbed his hands together, then leisurely moved towards his wife. He moved to stand directly behind Berlie, gently placing one hand on each shoulder. He looked directly at me and said, "Bette, this is my wife and the mother of my children. I love her, and I have no intentions of ever leaving her."

I stared at Ivan, saying nothing, then resumed glancing back down at his wife. Her eyes were cold and filled with pain. Ivan then moved to where I was sitting, he came behind my chair, and this time put one hand on each one of my shoulders. He looked at his wife in the eye and said, "Berlie, this is Bette. I love her like I have never loved any woman before, and I have no intentions of ever ending this relationship."

As I felt Ivan's hands leave my shoulders, a chill ran through my body. He moved back to the head of the table, an unexpected smile spreading across his face. "Now, ladies, why don't you two figure out the shit?"

Ivan turned and walked out of the dining room, leaving us alone with our reckless thoughts and simmering anger. At first, we just continued our silent standoff. Finally, Berlie broke the silence with a series of questions and demands, rattling them off like a machine gun.

"I understand you're married. With three children," she said in her best matter-of-fact tone.

"I am."

"And you love jazz. Is that right?"

I nodded.

"Has he taken you to hear any jazz yet?"

"Yes, he has."

I kept my head down, eyes on her hands, and wished this would end.

Berlie looked away, then back at me. Against my better judgment, I met her eyes, and the hurt I saw in them pierced my soul.

Before I could think of what to say, she issued her first demand.

"I want my husband home before 2:00 am," she said. I didn't answer, continuing my strategy of keeping quiet. I kept looking at her hands. No more eye contact; I could tell she wasn't a woman to be trifled with.

Suddenly, she lost her cool. "I guess you fuck better than I do!"

Her shout rattled me, but I didn't show it. Instead, I continued to hold my ground, saying nothing. With some people, silence had a way of hitting a nerve most words couldn't touch.

Berlie kept yelling. "I want the fucking to stop."

Ivan must have decided it was time to step in when he heard that, because there he was in the doorway. Looking at the two of us, he calmly said, "Ladies, I think you understand each other." "Obviously, we're not going to settle everything right here and now."

My heart was racing. Beads of sweat slipped from my arms. I wanted to scream, to tell Ivan that this wasn't right, that we needed to stop this madness, right here, right now. But I didn't. I couldn't. Whatever else happened, I would never risk losing him.

As if the room wasn't tense enough, Ivan took his spot at the head of the table, gave us equally stern looks, and announced, "Ladies… There's a jazz festival in Watts this Saturday. I'll be taking both of you with me."

I couldn't believe what I was hearing. He wanted to do *what?* Berlie and I had the same shocked face.

Without answering, I stood up and hoped my legs could carry me out the door. "I'll walk you to your car," Ivan hastily said, and stepped up next to me.

I shot his wife a faint smile and gave her a weak nod goodbye. Ivan and I walked out to my car. He gave me a soft kiss on my cheek and said, "I'll call you to make sure you got home safely."

I didn't say a word. I was still absorbing the conversation he'd thrust upon his wife and I. We all had a lot to digest, and talking would only have distracted from the process.

I drove home just as slowly as I had coming to the house. I was trying to process what I'd gotten myself into. I laughed out loud behind the wheel. It was all I could do to keep from crying.

If I was willing to put up with all this craziness, I told myself, I *must* really love him.

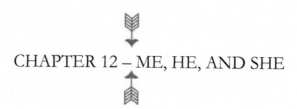

CHAPTER 12 – ME, HE, AND SHE

Saturday came in a blink of an eye. I was in no way ready, or willing, to publicly share Ivan with his wife, but after our conversation, it was pretty clear that was no longer my choice.

Ivan and Berlie arrived at my house precisely on time. I opened the door to reveal the couple standing in my entryway. Tense and quiet, I invited them into my home, greeting them both with a forced smile.

"Please, come in. Have a seat in the living room. May I get you something to drink?" I said in the politest voice I could muster.

Neither of them was thirsty. I was sure they were both just as nervous as I was, though I had to admit Ivan looked pretty calm and collected. His wife and I were dressed in a similar fashion. She wore a beautiful double-breasted beige suit with high heels, while I wore a white double-breasted suit with black heels. We both wore a natural hair style. I was starting to see why Ivan was attracted to me in the first place. Despite the color difference between his wife and me, Ivan definitely had a type.

We finally headed out into Ivan's car. I got into the backseat behind his wife; there was no need to ruffle any feathers with the seating arrangement. I knew my place, unspoken as it was.

When we arrived at the jazz festival, I started to sweat again. I'd been in awkward situations before, with the Adverb Party and the whole Betty Bang Bang business, but I was sure this took the cake. For me, at least; Ivan was standing tall with his head held high like an African king, not awkward in the least. The three of us entered the festival together, me on his left arm, Berlie on his right. The festival was packed, which didn't surprise me; it was a lovely celebration of music and multiculturalism, and we were surrounded by people from all over the city and around the world. Under any other circumstances, I'd have loved it.

As we made our entrance, we caught the eyes of various people, most of them no doubt trying to decipher what the hell was going on. I looked straight ahead, not giving them any attention. I never glanced over at Ivan's wife, but I'm sure, like me, she loved Ivan deeply and was willing to put up with his male ego to have both women on his arm.

That entrance is all I remember. I don't recall any of the music, who else we talked to, or when we finally left. It was as if I closed my eyes when we got to the festival and only opened them when the evening was over, as Ivan walked me to my front door.

Sleep eluded me that night. I lay awake, unable to wrap my mind around what just happened – or more importantly, *why* it happened. I had just gone out on a date with the love of my life *and his wife*. As I tossed it all around in my head, a thought came to me: *This isn't normal.* Couples – triples? – didn't go out and do this. This was something only Ivan Dixon himself could have devised.

The more I thought about it, the more I understood that it hadn't been a date at all. Ivan had succeeded with a plan. His purpose was to let everyone know that Berlie and I had full knowledge of each other. There would be no way for anyone to say anything that might catch her or me off guard. He'd done it to save us from any possible embarrassment, or so he thought.

We started seeing more and more of each other. As our lives grew closer together, I started to understand why Ivan wanted everyone's permission for us to date. The more time I spent dating a television actor, the more I saw that not only was his life an open book, but it also ran non-stop.

Ivan took me to a screening of *I Spy,* where I met Bill Cosby and his wife, Camille. We would also frequent the club where Bill Cosby performed in between shoots.

I was meeting producers, directors, and celebrities at every turn. His wife took care of the home and the kids, while I took care of him, always on his arm. His wife didn't complain, as far as I know, and I had nothing to complain about; this was the way he wanted it, and we both wanted to make him happy, so we acquiesced to his way.

Of course, his wife did have her own set of rules, one of them being that he be home before 2:00 am. One Saturday night, Ivan and I were out at the Lighthouse. Ivan wanted to hear a second set, but I knew it was time for him to go home. Needing a way to get him out of there, I lied, saying, "My nanny can't stay late. Please take me home now."

Ivan smiled, looked at me with his beautiful brown eyes, and said, "Of course. We should go."

When he dropped me off at Imperial, I got into my car and raced home. The first thing I did was run to my phone, glancing at the clock on the way – 1:30 am – and call his wife. Out of breath, I told her, "He's on his way home. If he doesn't get there before 2:00, he's not with me."

She responded like a kid. "Okay."

I hung up the phone and breathed a sigh of relief. I didn't mind one bit keeping my word to his wife, because for the first time in my adult life, I was happy and in love. Plus it gave his wife and I something to share. He didn't know about her rule; only she and I did. Keeping our agreement helped us build a little mutual trust, and kept us together in this strange arrangement.

CHAPTER 13 - CHICAGO

Ivan and I were fast becoming inseparable. When we were out and about on the town, I was the one they expected to see. One weekend, Ivan went to Chicago on business, and I missed him terribly. That was the first time in a long while I had gone more than a few days without seeing him. Early that Saturday morning, he gave me a call.

"I miss you so much."

I smiled, and my heart sang as I replied, "How much?"

Ivan laughed and said, "So much I wish you were here."

In that moment, my mind began to race. I told him, "Give me your telephone number. I'll call you back later."

I hung up the phone and immediately called United Airlines for a schedule to Chicago. The madness in my mind was telling me to leave LA and go surprise him. I didn't think; I just acted. I booked a 7:10 flight there, one way.

Next, I called Dada, my nanny. "Dada, I need you to stay overnight for two days until Monday. I'll be back late Monday night. I have to go out of town."

Dada never turned me down. She said, "Sure, I'll have my daughter bring me over right away."

It was set; I was going to surprise Ivan in Chicago. Just imagining his face when he saw me there made me light on my feet.

As I started dinner for the kids, I explained to them, "Mommy has to go away for two days. Dada is going to take care of you." There were no objections from any of them, as they loved Dada like their very own grandmother.

I anxiously waited for Dada to arrive, then packed my bags in the car and called George. He answered his private line after the first ring. As soon as I heard him pick up, I said, "My mother is ill, and I'm leaving for Maryland. Dada is here with the kids."

Bam! I hung up without giving him a chance to say a word. I bolted out the door to my car; I was on a mission, and no one was going to get in my way.

I arrived in Chicago's O'Hare Airport and headed for the first phone I saw. "Hello, Ivan? What's your hotel's name and address? I'm here! I'm right here at O'Hare."

There was complete silence on the other end.

I added, "I'm coming to visit you."

Very calmly, Ivan gave me the address to his hotel. Arriving there, I headed up to his room. As I rode the elevator, I almost had to pinch myself to make sure I was actually there, in Chicago, about to see Ivan.

I tapped on the door. Ivan opened it slowly. There was no smile, no hug, just a flat, "Hello. Let me take your coat."

Not knowing how to decipher Ivan's mood, I entered the room and sat on the couch. Two seconds later, the phone rang.

As Ivan answered, I held my breath and tried to listen. I heard him say, "Of course I love you. How are the boys, okay?" Then, as flat with her as he'd been with me, he ended the conversation with, "I'll be home on Monday."

Ivan slowly hung up the phone. It was as if Berlie had sensed that I was there with him. Slowly and sternly, he sat down next to me. Caught in the unexpected quiet, I was beginning to have second thoughts about my visit – until I heard him scream, "Bette, you are crazy, you know that?" He jumped up, grabbed me, and kissed me on the lips.

I beamed with delight at the explosion of excitement, matching his energy. "Well, you told me that you missed me, so here I am." We continued to embrace and kiss until we got our fill of each other.

Ivan got dressed, and we headed to the restaurant for a light late snack and cocktails. We chatted and gazed into each other's eyes for the next few hours, talking as if we hadn't seen each other in years. Was this what soulmates felt like?

Soulmates. I started to wonder. What else could you call the connection we had? Since our first date, Ivan had done things for me no man had ever done before. Intimate evenings at beautiful restaurants. Thoughtful gifts, without letting me pay for a thing. So many beautiful days together; no games, no drama, no pressure. Most of all, what we had together was mutual respect – or, as I'd come to call it, 50/50 love.

The next morning, we left for Cleveland. Ivan was attending an actor's workshop at the performing arts academy he'd attended before coming to Los Angeles. I stayed in the hotel.

Monday rolled around, and we left for the airport for LA. I had only purchased a one-way ticket to Chicago, so Ivan had to get a ticket for me to return home. As we approached the ticket agent, she needed proof that I was his wife. Ivan turned to me like a child, saying, "She needs proof that we're married." This was the first time that I saw the "little boy" in Ivan, unsure and insecure.

I stepped up and took his right hand, placing his credit card firmly in it and saying to him, "Put the credit card in front of her and say, 'Two tickets, one-way to LA, for Mr. and Mrs. Dixon.' Don't smile, just look firmly into her eyes."

I stood beside him, looking at the ticket agent with a firm expression. The agent knew what I was doing – I could tell by the way she rolled her eyes – but she didn't challenge our request. I smiled as I held onto Ivan's arm all the way to the departure gate.

Right before we boarded the plane, Ivan gave me a bigger smile than usual and said, "Bette, I didn't know you had it in you."

I was always so quiet with Ivan, never aggressive with him. He made me feel secure and feminine. In my marriage with George, I paid all the bills, including the office equipment, buying everything and ordering everything. I was clearly the man, mom, and dad to my children. It was nice to be the woman for once in a relationship, leaving the manly duties to the man.

When we reached LA, I had parked in a different area than Ivan's. We parted with a light kiss. "I'll call you as soon as I get home," he assured me.

The whole drive home, all I could think was that everything was going so well.

Too well. And I knew one thing about that: When you hit the top, there's nowhere to go but down.

CHAPTER 14 – HEART CONDITION

"I want to have lunch," said George.

"What?" I said into the phone.

"Today," he said, slower. "I want to come home from work and have a little tuna fish for lunch."

"Okay," I replied with a flat tone.

I asked Dada to put out some tuna fish with mayonnaise for Dr. Washington. Shortly after she did that, I was off to Hollywood to meet Ivan for a quick lunch. As I was leaving home, George was entering the cul-de-sac. We passed without saying one word to each other.

That evening, George called. "Today," he said, "when I came home, I was coming over to have lunch with you."

"Oh. You didn't say that. You said 'tuna fish.' I made tuna fish. You didn't say 'with me.'" I knew I was playing with semantics, but I also hoped I was making myself clear. I had no intentions of getting back with George. I was in love with a man who made me very happy. While Ivan had made it perfectly clear that he would never leave his wife, I cherished the time he and I spent together. So of course, George had to try to get back into my good graces again.

Never one to give up easily, George cleared his throat and asked, "What about going to the Rams game with me on Sunday?"

I thought about that for a minute. I never really saw Ivan on Sundays. He always took his oldest son to see the Rams game when they played in LA.

I considered the request and thought it might make for an interesting time. "Sure. We'll go to the game."

I hung up with George, then immediately called Ivan and asked, "Where do you sit when you go to the games?"

"I usually sit in the second level at the 80 yard line," Ivan told me. "Why?"

"I'll be at the game this Sunday," I said. "I'll look for you."

That was the first time I was ever excited about football. Game Day came quickly, and George and I soon took our seats in the stadium. When halftime rolled around, I told George I'd be back. I headed upstairs and towards the hot dog stand. To help Ivan spot me, I'd worn a bright yellow outfit that day.

As it turned out, I spotted him first, walking up through the oncoming crowd. His face lit up as we made eye contact, and he double-timed it through the crowd to reach me.

We flew into each other's arms, ignoring the crowd as it crushed past us. After a long, sweet kiss, he pulled back, nodded toward a passing vendor, and asked me, "Care for a hot dog?"

Rams games became our regular Sunday dates. We would never come to the stadium together, but we always found each other, no matter the size of the crowd. I'd wave, he'd wave, and we'd spot each other every time, just like that. Even there, even when the stands were packed with drunken fans or obnoxious kids, Ivan was a joy to be around and always made me feel like a queen.

As the weeks went by, I even found myself paying attention to the games themselves — until one game turned out to be a little more exciting than I cared for.

George and I were there at the stadium entrance, about to walk up to our seats, when George started walking more slowly and breathing more heavily. He turned away from the stairs, coughed once, and said, "I think I'll take the elevator."

Once we got to our seats, I asked him, "Are you okay?"

He gave me a faint smile. "I'm okay."

I didn't look for Ivan that game. I was too busy watching George. He was breathing through his mouth, rocking back and forth with each breath, but he kept insisting he was fine.

The game itself was the most exciting one we'd had all season. Our great defensive line — Rosey Grier, Merlin Olsen, Deacon Jones, and Lamar Lundy, aka the Fearsome Foursome — had everyone jumping to their feet with every phenomenal move they made. Everyone except for George. He just kept sitting there, staring at the game but not really watching it, brushing me off whenever I tried to take a closer look at him.

When the game was over, George haltingly handed me the car keys and told me to drive. The walk to the escalator took two or three times longer than usual, with George leaning on the railing all the way there.

By the time we reached the parking lot, and he dropped down on a bench and asked me to get the car for him, I had to ask: "George, are you having a heart attack?"

George didn't answer; he just looked at me and started to turn pale. That was enough for me. I ran to the car as fast as I could, which still took 20 minutes, as we'd parked a ways away. All the way there and back, I kept second-guessing myself. *Is he all right? What if he needs an ambulance? What am I doing?*

Finally, I got George home. By then, he could barely stand, so I immediately called a cardiologist we knew from our social circle. I told him about George's problem at the game. He urged me to get George to the VA Hospital in Long Beach immediately. He added that because George was a World War II veteran, his medical costs would be covered. Being a doctor, he used his "bedside manner" voice when he told me, "George has most likely had a heart attack."

I hung up the phone, turned to George, and said, "We need to get you to the VA Hospital." To my surprise, George refused to go, and nothing I said would convince him. Not knowing what else to do, I called his brother Ernest, who talked to George briefly on the phone, then told me he'd come down the next day. As George popped a few aspirin and rolled into bed, all I could do was sit and wait. Hour after hour crawled by, until Ernest finally arrived at the house early the next morning. I sat in the living room, listening to them argue, until Ernest finally dragged his brother out into the hall and told me, "We're going."

Once at the hospital, we learned that George was suffering from what's called, "congestive heart failure." Simply put, his heart was badly weakened, and was too seriously damaged for surgery.

"If you'd come in yesterday," the doctor told George as he pointed to a picture of his heart, "we might have had a chance to save all this damaged tissue. As it is, all we can do is stabilize your heart as much as possible."

The hospital admitted George for an extended stay. I knew someone would have to keep his practice running, so I called Dr. Whitmore, the medical doctor who owned the building where George had his office.

The following morning, I sat down in Dr. Whitmore's meeting room, bringing him up to speed on George. Since there was no telling how long George would be in the hospital, I needed to make sure the practice was well protected.

Dr. Whitmore was very empathic to our situation, and in short order, he assigned a Dr. Black to help fill in for George. Dr. Black was a young dentist, just starting out, but I had confidence he would be fine.

Unfortunately, after a week, he started having problems with two of the patients. The office was generally closed on Wednesday, and on Tuesday, all the late patients cancelled. That threw up a big red flag for me. I decided to take the patients' information to George so he could review it and make sure that Dr. Black was doing his job properly. We couldn't afford to have any more patients cancel.

When I arrived at the door of George's room, I saw a beautiful young woman sitting on the bed, holding George's hand. She had long brown hair that stopped midway down her back. A red short sleeveless dress showed off much of her cleavage. George had a puppy-dog look on his face as she softly talked to him and stroked his hand.

Neither one of them heard me coming into the room. I stood there for a moment, trying to figure out where I had seen this woman before. Then I remembered Jan's Beauty Salon. We were both clients there, and I had seen her several times.

Obviously, she wasn't George's first lover, but she was the youngest one I'd seen by far. As I later found out, she was a schoolteacher, just fresh out of college, and couldn't have been more that twenty-five years old. George had been up front with her about being married, but hadn't bothered to keep me in the loop.

I knocked twice on the open door before letting myself into the room. Neither of them looked up. She didn't even stop stroking his hand.

I walked up and calmly asked the young woman, "Will you leave for a minute? I need to speak with my husband."

Reasonable enough, I thought, but to my surprise, she didn't move. She just smiled at me and then back at George. I took a deep breath, trying to stay as calm as I possibly could. I returned her smile and said, "Listen, we don't have a marriage. This is business." I hefted a briefcase full of paperwork from the office. "I need to go over these patients' personal information with my husband, and then you can come back in."

George just sat there looking at her, almost like I wasn't even in the room. The woman held her ground and refused to move.

I felt my temper rising with each passing second. My hand squeezed tight on the handle of the briefcase. I took one last deep breath, and when she still didn't move, I slammed the briefcase against her pretty little head, sending her smashing against the wall. I heard her scream and George gasp. "What are you...?" he asked as he sat bolt upright.

I wasn't done. I pulled her up from the floor by her long brown hair. The young woman managed to wrestle out of my grip and bolt for the door. I turned and chased her down the hallway. The woman was screaming as if I was trying to kill her, which I was. She spun around the corner, busted through a set of double doors, and kept running down a long, wide corridor. I had to admit, she ran pretty damn fast in those heels.

I stayed hot on her trail, not letting her out of my sight, kicking off my shoes and continuing down what seemed like a never-ending hallway. Out of nowhere, I heard a nurse's voice scream, "Stop, Mrs. Washington, please!" As I turned to look behind me, there was George in his hospital gown, out of breath but doing his best to keep up. Behind him was the nurse, chasing him with an empty wheelchair.

By the time I got to the end of the hallway, I'd lost her. I finally stopped, out of breath. George caught up to me, eyes wide with exhaustion and amazement, and the nurse caught up to him. She carefully sat him down in the wheelchair, slapped an oxygen mask on his face, and immediately wheeled him off. I could still see his face gazing back at me, confused and ashamed.

Back in the waiting room, the nurse called to me. "Mrs. Washington, the doctor would like to see you."

I pulled myself together and told her I just needed a minute. Before I followed her, I called Jan's Beauty Salon. This wasn't over for me; I needed to make sure this woman knew I was serious.

I told Jan, the owner, what had happened. Jan let me know she was no longer welcome in her salon. "Mrs. Washington, I am so sorry. Everyone knew what was going on; we just didn't know how to tell you."

"That's okay," I said, still a bit out of breath. "I know now, and I'm going to end it once and for all. How can I get in touch with this woman?"

Jan then gave me the woman's phone number, which I called right away. The phone only rang once before the young woman's mother answered.

I spoke calmly and firmly. "This is Betty Washington, I am the wife of Dr. Washington, and the mother of his three children. I have just found out that your daughter is having an affair with my husband." The woman listened without saying a word.

"Now, I'm only going to say this once," I added, "I've already shot one woman. I don't want to shoot your daughter, unless I have to. He is ill. So tell her to stay away from him."

Her mother assured me that her daughter would never see Dr. Washington again. I hung up, retrieved my shoes from the hall, and made my way to the cardiologist's office. He invited me to sit down across from him, nodding to another, younger cardiologist, who stood facing me in the corner.

I took a seat while he filed away some paperwork. He gathered his thoughts, then looked up at me and said, "Mrs. Washington, I need to call Dr. Washington in to ask him some questions. I want you to listen and not say a word."

The nurse wheeled George into the room. The cardiologist looked at me, silently asking me to bite my tongue, then directed his attention to George. "Dr. Washington, what do you think of your wife's behavior today?"

George never looked at me; he just looked straight ahead and said, "She's crazy."

The doctor nodded gravely. "Why do you think she's crazy?"

"Did you see her?" George asked, chopping with his arm in my direction. "She could've broken the lady's jaw! She's *shot* people! Did you know that? She came right into my office with a gun. Damn near killed me once. Twice, now; I swear she's trying to give me another heart attack."

"Dr. Washington," said the older cardiologist, "you're the sole supporter of your wife and three children. She's been taking care of your business while you're here. She comes to see you, and there you are with another woman, sitting on the bed, holding hands. Your wife asks her to leave so she can speak to you about your patients, and your lady friend refuses to go. So, at that point, your wife explodes and chases the woman down the hall. Now, *you* just had a heart attack, and there you are, running after her, so the nurse has to stop you and put you in a wheelchair. And you say *she's* crazy?"

George turned to look at me, then turned back to the cardiologist. "She's always been crazy."

The doctor slowly shook his head, then nodded to his nurse. "Can you please take Dr. Washington back to his room? I'll be in to check on him in a few minutes."

The nurse followed directions and wheeled George away. Once he was out of earshot, the doctor leaned back and folded his arms. "Mrs. Washington, your husband is suffering from a delusional disorder. He would need years of therapy to come to terms with his illness, and with his heart the way it is, I really don't know if he'd live long enough for the treatment to run its course."

The cardiologist leaned forward in his chair. "I want to know what you are going to do now."

"Doctor, I have three children. I need to work in his office to keep the practice going; that's how our bills are paid." I wanted to let the doctor know that George's illness was his problem, not mine. My issue was keeping a roof over my head and my children fed and clothed; that was all. On that note, I stood up and added, "I promise I won't come back and cause you any problems."

With that, I turned and left the hospital. I never did get an answer on those patients.

CHAPTER 15 – THE SHADOW OF YOUR SMILE

I got a call two weeks later from Dr. Whitmore, inquiring if George could return to work. He was getting concerned about the office rent.

I suggested, "Ask him. I don't talk to George anymore." I figured I would spare him the story about the fiasco at the hospital.

That evening, Dr. Whitmore called me to let me know that George had been discharged a week ago. I was a little surprised to hear that. "Well, I have no idea where he is. I haven't seen him."

But by midnight, the doorbell rang. When I opened it, there stood Ernest with a male friend.

"Betty, my brother needs to come home to get well," Ernest said, pleading George's case. I said nothing as he continued, "I am not asking you to kiss his ass, but he needs to get well so he can support you and his family."

The friend standing next to Ernest spoke up and said, in a smooth and elegant voice, "Your husband seems to be consumed with the desire for sex. I found a collection of hardcore pornographic magazines under his desk and removed them."

Ernest continued. "Betty, if he only had one other woman, you'd have something to worry about. He doesn't, though. He has all kinds of women. He doesn't want to leave you for any of them. He just wants to come home to his family. Come home and get well."

I stood there without moving one muscle, listening to their plea. I surprised myself when I heard myself say, "He can come back tomorrow."

Ernest said, "He's outside in the car right now."

"Go get him," I said.

With a nod, Ernest turned around and walked back to his car. I watched as George walked in. He looked tired, underweight, and not nearly as good looking as he had been. Without so much as a hello, he shuffled down the hallway and into the bedroom, closing the door behind him as if nothing ever happened. He never even looked up at me.

A few minutes later, I entered the room to see George struggling to position his body between two pillows. With a deep sigh, I sat down next to him. He laid his head on my chest and went to sleep. I stayed awake, looking down at his face and thinking that I must be crazy - really crazy.

As I lay watching George asleep on my chest, I thought through my life. I had no degree, no money, and here he was lying helplessly on me like a baby. All the shit this man had done to me, and now, *now* I had to pity him. *I'll be damned.*

*****

George and I continued to co-exist in the home, but only for the sake of our children. I worked during the day in his office, while he stayed home to get well. After a few weeks of being at home, he started disappearing at night, always getting back before our nanny arrived in the morning. I never asked him any questions. I just didn't care anymore.

When the office work was light, I was able to leave and meet with Ivan. He and I would meet at one of our favorite eating places, a drive-in diner on Sunset and La Brea Boulevard. It had been three or four whole weeks since we'd seen each other last. Ivan had been away on a brief trip, but he would always make sure to call me every evening. We would talk for hours sometimes, just about our lives. He was a wonderful listener, always genuinely interested in what I had to say – unlike George, who was always thinking about something or somebody else.

One evening, in the car on the way to our favorite LA diner, Ivan turned on the radio. "The Shadow of your Smile" came on, from the Liz Taylor and Richard Burton movie *The Sandpiper*. We'd both seen the movie together, and as it turned out, we both loved that song. The two of us swayed back and forth while the tune hummed through the car speakers. As it ended, we screamed like teenagers and kissed passionately.

Of course, back then, cars had no CD players; we weren't even up to eight-tracks yet. But somehow, every time Ivan turned on the radio, we could always find a station playing "The Shadow of your Smile."

Once we even garnered the attention of a LAPD patrol car that was parked behind us. In the mist of our kissing, they honked at us. We turned around fast, only to see the officers giving us a hearty thumbs up.

No matter how much time I spent with Ivan, it was never enough. He'd drop me off outside the house, and by the time his car turned the corner, I'd be aching for his touch again. They say passion fades, especially when you're older, but with us, it grew every time. It's funny; I never really thought about what that might lead to.

One morning, as I was getting dressed for work, I felt queasy and heavy. At first, I thought it might be a late period, since I'd missed my last two – *Oh, God.*

That evening, I came home with a pregnancy test in hand. Sure enough, I was carrying my fourth child, and this one George had nothing to do with.

How was I going to tell Ivan?

I ran through the conversation in my head over and over again. Should I play it cool? Happy? Calm? How would he react? What about his wife? What would she say?

Did she own a gun?

The next time Ivan took me out, I asked him to take us to the diner again. Then, as we dug into our sandwiches, I said unmistakably, "Ivan, I am pregnant with your child."

He chewed the last bit of his BLT slowly and swallowed. Then a huge smile spread across his face. He touched my stomach and said, "Bette this is wonderful news! When... When, when are you due? Do you think it's a boy or a girl? Who do you think it'll look like, me or you?" My head began to spin. Ivan was reeling with excitement. Then in the mist of his excitement, his demeanor changed almost instantly. His arms stopped moving, his face fell, and he asked, "What type of man is George?"

"What do you mean?"

Ivan continued, "Is he responsible? Will he pay the money for his children?" I wasn't sure where he was going with that. Picking up on my confusion, he turned away and quietly said, "That's okay. That's my department." We didn't talk too much about the pregnancy after that. We just finished our dinner and headed home.

I tossed back and forth in bed all night. I thought about the confusion and uproar the child could bring – not just to our relationship, but to Ivan's career. I imagined his wife coming after me the way I had with the redhead. When the sun came up, I lay wide-eyed, barely breathing, and no closer to an answer. I only knew one thing: I had to make a decision quickly.

Two days later, I found a contact number for an abortion doctor. As happy as the news had made Ivan, having his child was just not the smart thing to do. I knew he'd try to talk me out of it, so I decided not to tell him until after the fact.

He might be angry, I knew, but I needed to go through with it for everyone's sake.

The doctor set the appointment for a week from the day I called. Knowing that seeing Ivan would make me think twice, and that I couldn't afford to change my mind, I avoided Ivan for that whole week. Then I drove to the doctor's office, had it done, and that was that.

Ivan and I saw each other a couple of times over the next few weeks, but not nearly as often as usual. Every time I moved, I felt the absence of the child, the life that had been growing inside me, the life I'd chosen to cut short.

Eventually, we went to see an Italian foreign film by Federico Fellini, called *Juliet of the Spirits*. The film was about an Italian woman finally getting free from her womanizing husband. It had these odd dream sequences, blurring the lines between farce and reality, and through all the abstract, artistic presentation, they spoke to me with so much heart and sincerity.

After the movie, we went to a motel. I sat on the bed, and Ivan got down on his knees to caress my stomach.

"Bette, when are you due?" he asked. "You're not growing."

My heart sank as I reached out and held his beautiful face. He was looking up at me with so much hope in his eyes and love in his heart. In that moment, I knew I had made a horrible decision. I took a deep breath and said, "Ivan, I had an abortion."

Ivan pulled away from me, sorrow filling his eyes. "Oh my God, Bette, why did you do it? Why? Why did you do it?" He turned around in circles, as if he didn't know what to do with himself.

He grabbed hold of his chair with both hands and swung his arms so hard he knocked over the small table next to me. He grabbed the small ashtray off the table and threw it violently, letting it rip a huge gash in the wall. I whimpered and cringed up into a ball at the corner of the bed. For the first time, I thought Ivan was going to hit me.

His outburst got the attention of the manager, who was only a few doors down from us on the first floor. I heard him bang on our door, screaming, "What the hell is going on in there!?"

The manager forced open the door with his key. He saw Ivan with his head in my lap, screaming, "Why, Bette? Why, Bette? Why did you do it!?"

I assured the manager that he was not hurting me and was only upset. The manager tossed a look around the room. "Anything you break, you bought it."

Ivan didn't reply. I looked at the manager. "We'll take care of the damages," I said. Satisfied, the manager turned and closed the door behind him.

I sat down next to Ivan, who was lying still across the bed, eyes fixed on the ceiling. I put my hand in his and I explained to him as best as I could, "Ivan, I know you wanted this baby... *Our* baby...but in the end, I knew we were both going to regret it. Especially you, with your career..." I knew my heart had to be aching as much as his.

Ivan's body shifted towards me. He looked into my eyes. I'd never seen him cry before. Tears rolled down his face, and I slowly wiped them away. "Please forgive me," I said. "I'm sorry I didn't tell you first."

Ivan reached out and embraced me tightly. I felt his sorrow with each breath he took. With tears still in his eyes, he pulled back and looked straight at me. "Bette, you have to promise me that if you get pregnant again, you will never, *ever* take the life of my child."

"I promise."

The rest of that night, Ivan and I held each other, mourning the child we could have had, the child who would never be a part of our lives.

CHAPTER 16 – EMPTY SHELL MARRIAGE

In my sociology major, I took a class called Social Problems. That class taught me the name and meaning of my marriage to George. The textbooks called it "The Empty Shell Marriage," when spouses remained legally married, but the marriage exists in name only. The two people live in the same household, but lead completely separate lives, with hardly any communication between them.

My attempt to discuss this with George fell on deaf ears. This was after I'd started filing for divorce, but before we'd finalized it, and he refused to discuss anything about it with me. Well, except when he tried to talk me out of it; sometimes he'd try to come up with alternatives to divorce, like, "If you want your boyfriend to come here, it's okay. He can park in the driveway, and when I come home and see his car, I'll go back to the office."

"I always thought you were crazy," I told him when he said that. "Now I know you're nuts."

My relationship with Ivan continued on as it had, despite the abortion and

George's antics. One day, Ivan called to invite me to the Monterey Jazz Festival. His voice sang as he went over the itinerary with me: "We can stay at Big Sur's Camping Ground, and drive up to Monterey for the festival. How does that sound?"

"Sounds great", I replied.

The Jazz Festival had the biggest crowd I'd ever seen. They were all there to see famous musicians, like Dizzy Gillespie and John Handy.

As Ivan and I approached the festival gate, I noticed people started staring and smiling at us. Everywhere I turned, people were looking and staring, staring and looking. It started getting to me. I finally stopped walking, turned to Ivan, and said, "Ivan, I can't do this."

Ivan gave me a puzzled look, "Do what, Bette? What's the problem?"

I didn't want to ruin our weekend together, but all the attention made me feel as if I were swimming in a fish bowl. I told Ivan, "All these people are staring at us because you're on TV."

Ivan burst into laughter. He slowly moved me over towards the gate, away from the flow of people heading into the festival. "You think they're looking at me?"

"Of course!"

Ivan dropped his head and chuckled. I wanted to tell him this was no laughing matter, but I didn't want to make our situation any worse.

Ivan then asked me, "Bette, hasn't George ever told you that you are beautiful?"

He hadn't, and I shyly shook my head.

Ivan gave me his smile, the one that always warmed me up inside. "Bette, you are a very beautiful woman. Look at you. Just a little bit of lipstick, and you *glow*. I am one proud king to have you on my arm. These people are looking at you, not me." He then gently took my hand and said, in a very comforting voice, "Come on, you can do this. They admire you, that's all."

Me, beautiful? I could hardly believe it. I grew up with my own grandmother telling me I would be okay if I weren't so dark. Ivan was the first man to let me know that dark-skinned was the epitome of beauty in his book, and that made me feel special.

I hadn't mentioned this before, but once we were inside the festival grounds, Ivan reminded me: Back on the set of *I Spy*, the casting director had once offered me the part of Ivan's wife, the queen to his African king.

"Do you remember what you told her?" he asked. I didn't, so he said, "You said, 'No thank you, I'm a student, not an actress.' And I loved that about you. I still do; you've got your own life and your own dreams, all independent of mine. That's wonderful. But Bette, even a *Hollywood casting director* thought you were beautiful. Good enough for TV! Now what do you say we forget about all the stares and enjoy the show?"

And we did.

After the festival, we headed to Big Sur and the Grand Canyon. For me, a woman from Baltimore, who'd never gone camping before, it was a beautiful new experience. Ivan must have really loved me; no man had ever done anything so romantic for me in my life. Over the next three days, we bonded like never before and took our love to a whole new level.

*****

Back in LA after the trip, Ivan asked me if I would go to a friend of his, a dress designer named Bob Rogers who made African clothing. "Bette," he asked, "would you wear an African dress if I had one made for you?" I could hear the excitement in his voice.

Ivan was very thoughtful and would buy me meaningful small gifts and other African clothes. I never needed much, since I had full access to my own household's money – George, even at his worst, trusted me with that – but the sincerity behind his gifts always warmed my heart.

"Sure," I said.

Ivan got me the address to Bob Rogers' studio and said he'd make an appointment for the next week. I met Bob the following Wednesday. The first thing I noticed about Bob was his funny walk. I guess he caught me staring, because he turned to me and said, "I'm gay."

"So what?" I responded, and we both chuckled.

That broke the ice. Bob took my measurements and had me select several fabrics and colors from an overwhelming number of choices. I decided on a certain colored fabric, with orange and chocolate browns woven into the pattern. It was the best looking fabric for my skin tone; I would have chosen blue, but there was nothing in the blue fabric with a solid color.

Over an hour went by in the studio. I was running late for my class, so I quickly grabbed my purse started toward the door. I heard Bob yelling behind me, "Wait, you also have to choose a style."

I yelled back at him, "Aren't you the designer? You choose the style." And with that, I was gone, leaving Bob to do what Bob did best.

I must have left an impression on him, because Ivan called me that evening and said, "Bob told me if he wasn't gay, you would be a woman he could fall in love with." I smiled at that, although the only man I wanted to be with was Ivan.

Two weeks later, Bob called to say the dress was finished. I headed over to see what he had designed for me. To my amazement, Bob had created *two* beautiful dresses. They were both long, with the arms completely covered, one a V-neck, and the other squared. I was in love with them both.

I decided to wear one of the dresses out one night when Ivan and I hit one of our favorite jazz clubs on Sunset. I felt like his queen in my finest regalia. George would have never volunteered to buy me anything that uplifted me that way. All he did was find ways to bring me down. Throughout the evening, Ivan socialized with his friends, but always did his best to include me. That night, we rented a hotel room and made love. I never knew I could fall so hard for one person, but each day brought more joy my way, and I couldn't see myself ever being without

him.

Me in Big Sir, California. This photo was taken by Ivan.

CHAPTER 17 - THE FINAL WAR OF OLLY WINTER

Ivan was in his acting prime. As soon as he was done with one show or movie, his agent had another job lined up. His fame and notoriety were growing, and I couldn't have been more proud.

In 1967, Ivan landed the title role in a TV special called *The Final War of Olly Winter*. The shooting was at CBS Studios on Fairfax, where I visited him several times a week. Ivan was always very busy when I was there, so I tried not to bother him much, giving him his space to relax and prepare for his scenes.

One day, Ivan had a small break in his shooting, so he suggested that we take a little private lunch over at the Farmer's Market, a Los Angeles landmark and tourist attraction combining food and fun. I was thrilled; having Ivan all to myself was rare when he was shooting. We were there at the market, eating Chinese food, when the director of the special appeared.

"Hey, Ivan, I need to speak to you about a scene."

I shocked myself, and was pretty sure I even surprised Ivan, when I said,

"Please, can I have him all to myself for at least thirty minutes?"

The director looked at me, then at Ivan, who was smiling from ear to ear. "Sure. Ivan, I'll see you back at the set then."

I was a little embarrassed for voicing my feelings, but I wanted to spend time with the man I loved. We continued to eat lunch in comfortable silence; just being in each other's presence was good enough for us. I looked up to take a peek at Ivan, who was mixing his food and smiling, looking like he was waiting for me to speak. I just smiled back and ate my sweet and sour pork and fried rice.

When we both finished, Ivan wiped his mouth and said, "Bette, is there anything else you'd like?"

Without looking directly at him, I said, "No."

We stood up together. Ivan reached out to adjust the collar of my summer blouse and softly said, "You drive carefully. I'll call you this evening." He then kissed me gently on my forehead and walked me to my car.

All the way home, I couldn't stop smiling.

I decided to go down to the set on the final day of shooting for the *Ollie Winter* special. I watched a love scene between Ivan and a beautiful Asian woman. It was interesting seeing how they shot it, since I had only seen love scenes while watching movies in the theaters. This was totally different, the movies don't show how the actors are surrounded by lights and cables and all this other equipment, with crew members standing just off camera. The film industry fascinated me; although I had no desire ever to be an actor, it was a lot of fun seeing how it was done.

As I stood watching the love scene between Ivan and his Asian co-star, a cameraman came over to me and said, "How do you feel seeing your man making love with another woman?"

I wasn't sure if he was trying to provoke me, but if so, he was barking up the wrong tree. I quickly told him, "He's working. He doesn't kiss me like that. There's no passion in that kiss, none at all." The guy gave me a funny look, turned and walked away. Maybe he didn't like my response, or was looking for something different. It didn't matter.

Ivan and I ended up spending the night together in a nearby hotel. I could tell that Ivan was exhausted from the long day of shooting, and the few drinks we'd had at the bar down the street hadn't exactly perked him up either.

Once we got into the room, Ivan tumbled right into bed. With his eyes half open, he laughed and said, "You'd better hurry and get whatever you want before I pass out." Before I could even completely undress, he was fast asleep. I put on my nightgown, took off Ivan's shoes and socks, and made him comfortable. Then I wiggled into the crook of his arm, where I felt very safe, and went straight to sleep.

The next morning, Ivan woke with a huge smile on his face and asked, "Did I fall asleep on you last night?"

I kissed Ivan softly on his cheek. "That just gave me more time to lie in your arms." I giggled as he gave me a satisfied nod.

CHAPTER 18 – THE NEW TESTAMENT

During my second year at Pepperdine, I had to take a course in Religion on the New Testament. Up to that point, I'd gone through the motions with the school's religious material, but that one course… Well, it changed my life.

The Old Testament was full of laws and covenants. Most of its stories were all about famine, plagues, wars, incest, and slavery. I understood it all, especially since the courses helped me analyze the language, but I never had much interest, since so little of it had anything to do with my own life.

On the other hand, The New Testament held a whole different philosophy. In particular, the teachings of Christ, about how to live life every day, were just as relevant to me as they ever had been. The Sermon on the Mount, the Beatitudes, and many other lessons all stated simple principles of right and wrong. There was no getting away from the truth of them, and some of that truth was hard for me to reconcile.

A passage from the Gospel of Matthew jumped out at me first: "No one can be a slave of two masters: he will either hate the first and love the second, or treat the first with respect and the second with scorn. You cannot be a slave to both God and money." In essence, that meant I couldn't straddle the fence the way I had been. I was living wrong, thinking it would make me happy. In reality, only half my life was happy, and the other half was miserable.

And just as I rationalized one part of the text, another verse would pop up for me to tackle. "So always treat others as you would like them to treat you; that is the meaning of the Law and the Prophets." The only difference between myself and George's other women was that Berlie knew who her husband was having an affair with, while I was in the dark.

Regardless of that one difference, I was doing wrong to Berlie, even if I was trying to compensate by making Ivan as happy as I could. The Scriptures started working on my head and traveling toward my heart. And that wasn't all happy or easy; that course was hard work, and it wasn't the only course I had that semester. As my school obligations piled up, I started getting irritable, missing deadlines, and forgetting simple tasks. I felt like I was racing to a finish line without the proper shoes. Each step I took was a struggle, but I was determined to finish.

Because I'd decided to increase my class load to a full schedule, I was studying around the clock. I constantly reminded myself that education was my ticket to my freedom, independence and self-worth. I recruited a few ladies and formed a study group so that we could help one another stay on schedule.

George came home one night around 1:00 am to find us with our noses in our books. When the ladies left, he asked, "Why such heavy studying?"

"We've got a midterm coming up."

"How many classes are you taking?"

"Four," I said, instantly regretting it. I should have lied to him.

"Why the full course load? What's the rush?" he asked.

I looked up at George and decided to tell him the truth, no matter how he took it. "I'm getting my degree, and when I'm finished, I want to finalize the divorce. I won't live like this anymore." George listened, but didn't say a word.

He needed to hear what was on my mind, so I asked him, "Do you remember when Valerie told you, 'Daddy, you don't love my mommy'; then she turned to me and said, 'Mommy, you don't love daddy'?"

George slowly nodded his head.

"That was a hard blow coming from a child, but it was the truth. We are done, George, and the sooner I get this degree, the sooner you will be out of my life."

George looked down at me and deadpanned, "Buddy, you'll never get that degree."

"I will," I said. "I need it, and I'm getting it."

George turned away and said, "If I had wanted an educated woman, I would have married one."

When I heard those words escape George's mouth, my entire body tensed. I felt my rage building up inside of me like a volcano ready to erupt.

"Is that so? You wanted me because you thought I was stupid. You thought you were smarter than me. You know what your mother told me? She thought you were going to marry some DC elementary school teacher, but you married me, a woman with an elementary school education.

"But let me tell you one thing: This less-than-educated woman is the best thing that could have happened to your candy ass! I sacrificed and delayed my life to support you and pay *your* way through dental school. They wouldn't even have let you *into* dental school if I hadn't stuck up for you! I had your babies, and I put up with your shit. So yes, it's my time now to get what *I* deserve, and *my* education, which it's *your* turn to pay for, is my one-way ticket away from you!"

He had nothing to say to that.

The next day, I went to talk to his brother's ex-wife, Rosemarie. Now that she'd divorced Ernest, I felt comfortable confiding in her about my problems. Her suggestion was simple: "Just finish your divorce, get your alimony, and do what you want with your money."

Since Rosemary had been at home with my kids and me when George had come in at all hours of the morning, she agreed to be my witness. She even gave me the name of her attorney, Charles Matthews.

Unfortunately, George still didn't care to cooperate. First, I asked him to leave the home, but he refused. Next, I repeatedly gave George the address to the attorney's office on Crenshaw, since George had to go in and sign the papers. When I followed up with the attorney, he told me that George had kept skipping out on his appointments.

The constant frustration took its toll. My grades started slipping. I stepped on the scale and realized I'd lost fifteen pounds. Even the professor of my New Testament class, Professor Reynolds, took notice, asking me to stay after lecture one day.

The Professor was a Protestant minister. He looked young, but he was an old soul, and his eyes seemed to look right through you, just as easily as they looked through his thick-rimmed glasses.

I was one of the few students in his class over the age of twenty, and I'm proud to say I was also one of the most dedicated. Where other students would write two-page essays, mine were always at least five or six pages. This was the first time he'd asked to speak with me one-on-one; I just wished it had been under better circumstances.

"Mrs. Washington," he asked me point blank, "am I saying anything that conflicts with your Catholicism?"

"I'm having marital problems," I told him. "But I plan on seeing a priest for confession."

"That's a good first step," he said with a nod. "Confession is good for the soul. At least, it can be. But it's hard sometimes. We don't have confession here the way you do, but people do come to me. They confess, and some people hope that's enough to fix their problems. Trouble is, just talking about your problems doesn't always fix them. It can tell you *how* to fix them, but that's when you have to get up and *do* something."

He turned and gathered up his notes. "Now, listen, Betty, you're a great student, and I'd hate to see you fall behind. Obviously, I can't take your confession, but if you have any questions, if there's any advice I can give you, please feel free to come talk to me."

"Thank you, Professor Reynolds," I said. Not knowing what else to do, I gathered my books and headed out.

He had a point, and I started worrying about what the priest might say. He'd condemn my sins for sure, but what I worried about most was what he might ask me to do.

Regardless, I decided to go to confession that Saturday at Transfiguration Catholic Church. It was the beginning of Lenten season, so the lines were very long. After at least an hour, I made it up to the confessional, closed the curtains, and waited for the priest to slide open his window. As I sat there in the dark, my mind started running at top speed, trying to predict the conversation ahead. Every second I waited, I ran through every word of it again, differently each time.

Finally, the priest slid his window open. I bowed my head and said, "Forgive me, Father, for I have sinned. I cannot remember when my last confession was."

"What is your sin, my child?"

I took a deep breath, then explained everything that was going on in my life. I outlined my relationship with George, then told the priest all about my affair with Ivan, how he paid me attention, and treated me like a worthwhile person, and made me happier than anyone.

The priest listened quietly throughout the whole story. When I finished, he paused for just a moment, then told me, "You must commit yourself to never seeing this man again. Give him up. Give up the relationship, for the sanctity of your marriage and your soul."

Just the thought of leaving Ivan twisted my stomach into a knot. "Father," I said, "I cannot do that. I cannot give him up."

"Then I cannot give you absolution. You need to make an appointment to come for counseling. Surely, you must know what you are doing is wrong, and staying in this relationship will not bring you peace."

I walked out of that confessional feeling dazed and confused. Leaving the church, I wandered through the parking lot until I found my car, then started driving aimlessly. The priest's words kept ringing in my head. *Give him up. Give up the relationship.*

I shouted, "NO!" as loud as I could.

I drove fast down Santa Barbara Boulevard, heading towards the freeway. I didn't realize just how fast I was going until I saw the lights and heard the sirens of a motorcycle cop right behind me.

As the officer handed me the ticket, all the pain, confusion, and stress boiled up at once, pouring out of my eyes in long, hot tears.

The officer looked at me and said, "Ma'am, this is just a ticket. You're not going to jail, though I have to say with the way you were driving, you oughtta be locked up." I started to cry harder.

He took pity and asked, "Miss, what's the problem?"

I pulled myself together and told him how the priest had refused to give me absolution.

The officer took a deep breath and softened his tone. "I'm sorry to hear that, but I can't tear up the ticket. What I can do is escort you to the freeway." With that, the officer jumped back on his motorcycle. I trailed him to the freeway at 35 miles an hour.

*****

Despite what the priest said, I continued to see Ivan.

On a few occasions, when Dada could stay over to watch the sleeping kids, I went to Culver City at night. During Ivan's film shoots, I would study in his trailer. Between all the running back and forth to see Ivan, the stress George was putting on me by not signing the divorce papers, and the words of the priest still dancing in my head, I started getting more and more easily agitated, uncontrollably so. I'd snap at the slightest things, to the point where even Ivan noticed.

It came to a head one Saturday afternoon when we went to a beach motel in Malibu. I'd bought a new record player so we could lay back and listen to some jazz, but it wouldn't work; no matter how I plugged it in or which buttons I pressed, nothing happened. I slammed it down on the dresser three times, and when that didn't fix it, I called the store right from the room and cursed the man who sold it to me. Then I ordered him to get his manager, and I raged at him too.

Ivan stood up from the bed, took the phone gently but firmly, and eased it out of my hand. "I'm sorry," he told the man. "I'll bring this record player back to you on Monday, all right? Let me take care of this." He hung up and sat in a chair, looking at the beach with his head in his hands.

After taking a breath, he lifted his eyes up to me. I could see the disappointment all over him. "Bette, what's wrong? What's the matter?" My anger evaporated, leaving only silence in its wake.

Ivan snapped his fingers. "We need some fresh air. Some food, and then maybe I should give you a ride to your car," he said. "Unless you can spend the night, you might want to go home and rest. Have you got the receipt for that record player?"

I huffed and started going through my purse. "Somewhere, I think. Look, I don't think I can stay, so… I'm not very hungry either…" With that, I slowly got up, gathered my things, gave him the receipt, and left.

That was the first time Ivan had ever seen me out of character. I wasn't proud of my behavior at all. Everything seemed to be closing in on me too fast, and I didn't know where to turn.

Part of the problem was that I hadn't actually told Ivan I was divorcing

George – so, of course, I hadn't told him George wouldn't sign the papers either.

I didn't want to get Ivan's hopes up, or cause any more trouble with Berlie. So I

just   kept   quiet,   and   it   boiled   and   boiled   inside   me.

CHAPTER 19 – NO MORE COOLING OFF

No more.

No more of George's stubborn, manipulative ways.

No more of George, period.

I called my attorney and told him I'd be bringing George in the next day, come hell or high water. I asked him how late we could get there to sign the papers. He told me 7:30 pm at the latest.

When I hung up the phone, it rang again immediately. I thought about leaving it and grabbing George right then, but I stopped and picked it up.

"Bette?" Ivan said from the other end. "I was just calling to check up on you. Are you all right?"

Just hearing Ivan's voice released a calm wave all through my body. I sat down and crossed my legs. "I've been better."

I knew he deserved to know why I'd been in such a terrible state of mind, whether I wanted to tell him about it or not. I took a deep breath. "Ivan, I'm filing for divorce, and I'm having trouble with George. He refuses to move out or sign the papers."

Ivan was quiet. "Well, I knew it had to be something."

My voice started to tremble with each word that escaped. "I'm so sorry, Ivan. I've been under so much stress. My exams, all this craziness with George... It's just been too much for me."

"You don't need to apologize. It's okay." He chuckled. "I returned the record player and got you a new one. Bette, meet me for lunch. I want to see you."

I wanted to say yes, but I knew I had to take care of business with George first; I couldn't let it go one more minute, "I can't, at least not right now. I'll call you when I can, and I'll see you when I can, okay?"

He said, "Okay, I'll be waiting."

I could hear the disappointment in Ivan's voice, but at the same time, I think he knew it was for the best. With a small sense of relief, I hung up the phone. Now that Ivan knew what I'd been going through and what my next steps were, those steps felt much more real. I was finally ready to close a major chapter in my life.

The next evening, I went to the dentist's office around 6:00 pm. George had just one patient, in the first cubicle. I gently took the bib off of her and told her to leave. Next, I told the secretary she could go home, so she quickly stood up and headed out the door. I walked down the hallway towards George's office, but before I entered, I pulled out my gun, made sure it was loaded, and then reached for the door.

George heard the door open, looked up, and saw the gun. He opened his eyes wide and pounded the desk. "Are you crazy?!!"

I calmly walked over to where he sat and said, "I don't want any problems. The attorney is waiting for us to come sign the papers…together, no more missing appointments. So get your jacket and let's go."

This was it. This was the moment I took back control. I felt *alive* for the first time in years. I felt like my blood was electrified. I was trembling so much I nearly pulled the trigger by accident more than once. But I got George to the attorney's office with his head intact, and with three hours to spare.

When we got to the office door, George walked in front of me. I kept just a few steps behind him, just farther back than he could reach, with the gun still out. As we stepped inside, Matthews the attorney saw the gun, jumped up from his desk, and yelled, "Whoa, is that thing loaded?"

"Of course," I told him. "How else did you expect me to get him down here?"

Matthews frowned in disapproval. "Mrs. Washington, please give me that gun." I looked at George, then handed the gun over. The attorney whisked the bullets out of it and set the gun down on his desk.

"We need to have a cooling off period," the attorney said.

"No," I told him. "No. No more 'cooling off.' I'm finished."

George interjected. "She's the one who wants the divorce, not me."

I swiveled in my seat toward my soon-to-be-ex-husband and said, "You have driven me *straight* to this divorce since the day I married you. Not once have you ever been a husband to me."

I could feel the tension from both the men in the room. The attorney discreetly brushed the gun and the bullets a little farther apart.

"Please, let's all just...take a moment," said Matthews. He looked at me, pursed his lips, and then spoke again. "I divorced and married the same woman twice. It cost a fortune. So before you go through with this, you need to be absolutely sure about every single part of it."

I understood what the attorney was trying to do; he wanted to make sure we were finally done. But, he didn't know me, and he didn't know George. If he had, he'd have understood that we'd reached our final conclusion. So I explained it to him.

"We had a legal separation in 1962. I got pregnant, we had our second daughter, and he never stopped cheating, womanizing, whoring around—"

Matthews stashed the gun and bullets in separate drawers.

Undeterred, I plowed on. "He had a woman sleep in *our* bed *while* I was in the hospital giving birth. Now he wants me to drop out of school! He married me because he thought I was ignorant. I *was* ignorant," I corrected myself, "especially about him. But no more. No more! I have been 'cooling off' for over ten years. I'm done, and you'd better believe it."

"Good enough," said the attorney. He pushed a stack of papers toward George. It took all of two minutes for George to sign those papers, and when it was finally all said and done, I felt a rush of relief cascade through my body.

"I'm keeping this gun for a few days," said the attorney.

That was fine with me. I told the attorney that George could come to my home tomorrow to get the remainder of his clothes. I suggested that he do so during the day, when Valerie and Gregory were in school. I also informed George that I'd already had the locks changed, so he shouldn't bother bringing his keys.

Matthews went over the last bit of information concerning our divorce, including the fact that George had agreed to pay $1500 in alimony and child support on the fifth of every month.

We left and drove back to George's office in silence. George got out of the car and closed the door, never saying one word to me.

CHAPTER 20 – REWRITING THE SCRIPT

Matthews was right. Divorce was costly. In fact, when George signed those divorce papers, he also signed me over to financial hell.

It started when I lost control of all the money, including my Diners' Club and Sears cards. George got the whole dental practice, with all the expenses and revenue that came with it. I got the house, just like I wanted, but that came with a hefty mortgage. That Cadillac wasn't paid off yet, either.

Oh, and that $1500 a month? Not even close. George paid me in $100 and $200 dribbles, when he bothered paying me at all. I tried to sic Matthews on him, but George kept feeding him some line about being broke, always promising to pay me "as soon as he could." He had nothing for the nanny, nothing for Gregory and Valerie's school, nothing but excuses. If that was his way of getting back at me, he was lower than I'd ever thought. My attorney said he'd work to get George into court, but that would take time, more time than I had.

I had an aunt when I was younger who'd always told me to squirrel away money in my own account, no matter what happened. I should've listened to her, but I never did, and I spent all night almost every night kicking myself for that.

First, they came for the furniture. My floor model television set was repossessed. Then my beautiful home was threatened with foreclosure. By the second month, I had to hock my diamond ring to put food on the table for my children.

I'd honestly thought George's signature would be the end of my worries. I'd been so wrapped up in his stalling and bitching that I hadn't thought past it at all. Now, there I was, fallen, riches to rags. It broke me down, day by day.

I lay back one night, after having finally gotten the kids down for bed. My stomach was growling, but I'd managed to scrape together leftover rice and beans for them, at least.

I closed my eyes, forcing back my tears, not giving George that satisfaction, even though he couldn't see me. I took a deep breath as I reached for the phone sitting on the end table, placing it in my lap. The last thing I'd wanted to do was beg Ivan for help, but George had left me no choice. Another few days, and I'd have found myself on the streets with three children. I picked up the receiver and dialed Ivan's number.

When Ivan answered the phone, my emotions got the best of me; they came crashing down like a wave onto the shorefront. Then, as Ivan's voiced calmed my soul, I pulled myself together.

I sat back and said in a shaky voice, "George is trying to force me to take him back by withholding the alimony and child support. I refuse to take him back. I am down to nothing, but I have to wait for my attorney to get him back in court."

Ivan listened quietly, then said, "Don't worry. Tell me what you need, and I'll bring it to you after I get off of work."

I began to cry, as quietly as I could. As tears streamed down my face, I told Ivan how embarrassed I was to have to ask him for financial help.

"Don't worry, Bette. I will bring you the money."

I slowly hung up the phone and continued to cry, but with relief this time. Relief, and a deep love for such a blessing of a man.

Several hours passed. I was still sitting in my chair when the doorbell rang. I stood and quickly fixed my clothes and hair as much as I could before the bell rang again. When I opened the door, I was shocked to see not Ivan, but *Berlie*.

She looked very sad, and was shaking a bit. I asked her, "What in the world are you doing here?"

Ivan's wife didn't answer right away, but stepped straight into my home. She looked down at the floor, then at me. "I rewrote the script," she said.

"What do you mean?"

Her eyes started filling with tears. "I was supposed to refuse to bring you the money, but I knew that would make him threaten divorce. So I gave Ivan a big surprise when I agreed to bring it to you."

I was silent, not knowing what to say. I felt her hurt and fear with every word that escaped from her shaking lips.

"You don't have to ask Ivan for help. Call *me*, and I will give you whatever you need for you and your children." Her head dropped once again. She began to sob. "Please don't take my husband."

"Take him?" I repeated. "From you? No, I…" I trailed off as she gave another long, pained sob.

"Please don't take my husband," she said again. "He wants you, not me."

I held silent, just breathing. Then I finally reached out and touched her shoulder. "Listen – Berlie, look at me. My divorce has *nothing* to do with Ivan. My marriage was over way before I ever *met* Ivan. You have to understand that. I am not trying to take your husband."

She shook her head, as if we were speaking two different languages. "Ivan doesn't see it that way. He thinks he has to make a choice. Your being single makes it different."

I didn't know how to make her understand, make her see that I never intended to take him away from her. Our love, our 50/50 love, it just happened; it was out of our control. But how could I possibly explain that?

Then I thought of something. "Berlie, if I wanted to take your husband I could have done it a year ago. I got pregnant. I had an abortion. I didn't want anything to ruin what you had with him. I didn't even tell Ivan about the abortion until it was all over. He was mad! I'd never seen him so angry. But I couldn't do that to you. Not to your marriage or your family."

Berlie's cries turned to full-blown hysterics. I was at a complete loss. She headed over to a chair, at a snail's pace, and sat down. She buried her face in her hands and continued to sob uncontrollably.

I walked over and sat down next to her, "Why are you crying now? I'm just trying to tell you, I am *not trying to take your husband*."

With her makeup running down her cheeks and her eyes bloodshot, she looked up at me again. "Ivan once told me that if any woman ever killed his child, he would never have anything to do with her again. He told me that."

Well, great.

"Now I *know* he wants you and not me. Just please don't take him away."

The phone rang, breaking our connection, making me wonder who could be calling. My friend Della, who was a guest that night, answered the phone. She came into living room, gave Berlie a quick, awkward glance, and told me, "For you."

It was Ivan on the phone; I knew it. I stood and headed to the kitchen. When I picked up the receiver, I didn't say *Hello* or *How are you*; I simply said, "Why did you do this?

Ivan carefully responded, "I don't understand. I want you to have what you need."

I continued, "Ivan, why would you have her bring me the money? Why would you degrade her womanhood this way? It's humiliating. Can't you see that?"

There was silence on the other end. I dropped my head in pure shame and embarrassment for Berlie. Then I heard Ivan's voice simply say, "Bette, please put my wife on the phone."

I called Berlie into the kitchen. She was still crying as she slowly took the phone out of my hands and placed it to her ear. I watched her talk with Ivan. Her only responses on the phone were three soft, "Okays." I felt her sadness radiate out from her body.

I swallowed hard. With nowhere else to go, I stayed in front of Ivan's wife, racked with pain, as she pleaded for the man who was legally hers, but emotionally mine. I knew in that moment that I had to make a decision. I thought back to what the priest told me, and it all made sense now. I couldn't continue to live like this. Only hurt would come of it; only despair would be the victor.

Once we were back in the living room, I turned to her and said, "Look at me. Berlie, look me in the eye. …It's finished."

She blinked as if she didn't understand. I told her, "You don't have me to worry about me anymore. I promise you I will never see him again. The relationship is over. Please believe me. It's over."

Ivan's wife just stood there, nodding her head. Her face was still filled with sadness as I walked her to my front door. She headed out, then turned back one last time. We locked eyes, neither of us uttering a word. We didn't have to. It truly was over. I watched as Berlie headed out of the driveway and out of my life.

I closed the door, leaned against it, and began to cry myself.

Della walked over to me with anger on her face. "You are the biggest fool! That man wants you more than his own wife, and you just promised her you were never going to see him again!"

I pulled myself together and responded, "Della, how can I have any happiness with him when she's so miserable? I can't build *my* happiness on *her* unhappiness. It just wouldn't work. I don't want George, but that doesn't make it right to go after her husband. He's hers, not mine. She loves him. I have to respect that. I have to respect their marriage."

With my head pounding and a dizziness creeping over me, I headed up to my bedroom to lie down. As I walked down the hallway, I felt Della watching me with disdain. I don't know if she heard me say, "I made her a promise, and I will keep that promise."

I stepped into my room, shut the door, and cried until I couldn't cry anymore.

CHAPTER 21 - BREAKDOWN

I paid dearly for giving up Ivan.

Being with him all that time had been so wonderful, had lit up my life so completely, that I'd never really considered the consequences. I was dating a married man, as a married woman, and now, for violating that sacred institution twice over, it was payback time.

First, his absence hit me physically. After just a few days without him, I started feeling ill. My body ached from head to toe, and I couldn't keep anything down. Minutes seemed like hours and hours seemed a lifetime. I walked like a zombie, never looking at myself in the mirror as I went through my day.

One afternoon, when I returned home from picking up Valerie and Gregory, I finally glanced at myself in the hallway mirror on the way into the kitchen. I was shocked to see that I had forgotten to change out of my bathrobe or to rub in the lipstick that I used as rouge on my cheeks. I looked like a circus act. For a woman who was always put together, a woman who loved fashion, I was losing it in every way.

It wasn't long before sleep became my enemy. I found myself up most of the night, my mind racing a mile a minute with Ivan at the forefront of my thoughts. The next day after the robe incident, as I was driving down La Brea, I fell asleep at the wheel and rear-ended the trunk of an Oldsmobile.

Thank God no one was hurt. My Cadillac wasn't so lucky. I managed to get the car fixed, but Della had to escort me and the kids around for the next few weeks.

My mental state kept on slipping. Just getting through each day became a ridiculous challenge. Living my life void of Ivan was a constant struggle, harder than I'd ever imagined.

I was home alone one afternoon when I began hearing a conversation between a man and woman. I walked to the back door to see if my neighbors were outside talking a little too loud, but when I stepped outside, there was no one to be found. I headed back inside to make sure I hadn't left the radio or the TV in the kitchen on by mistake. Both were off. The voices continued as I searched the house, checking through every window, behind every door, even tearing the covers off the bed.

Twenty minutes later, I knew I couldn't deny it anymore; the voices were coming from inside my head. And they didn't stop. I could only barely make out the words, but those words kept on coming. I couldn't concentrate, couldn't sleep; the best I could do, over the next few days, was learn to calm them down a bit. Calm or not, they still wouldn't stop.

I felt myself slipping down a dark, inescapable hole. The voices turned to ghosts, hallucinations right in front of my eyes. Blurry, like visual echoes through a frosted glass door, but always there, just out of my reach. I started to believe that Ivan was coming over to see me. I sat in my usual chair; waiting for him to come to my aid, to tell me that everything was going to be okay. I needed to feel his touch, hear his voice, kiss his lips.

And there I sat, for hours and hours, knowing I wouldn't have to get up to let him in. Knowing he'd just walk right on through the door and sweep me off my feet.

My mind wandered as I waited there, through hopes and fears and memories. I saw myself on the cliff again, dancing by myself this time, spinning closer and closer to that deadly plunge, but knowing that he'd be there to save me.

And in the very back of my mind, a little spark sent out a signal, warning me that the last shred of my sanity was about to burn away.

Just then, the phone rang. It had to be him. Had something come up? I crossed the room and snatched up the receiver. "Ivan! Where are you?"

"Betty? It's Rosemarie."

Rosemarie, Rosemarie... Oh, right, George's brother's ex-wife. What did she want with me?

"Listen, are you okay?" she asked. "I've been talking to Della, and, well, have you talked to Ivan lately?"

"Oh, I'm expecting him any minute," I told her. "He's right about to walk through the door."

"Through the door," she said, her voice flat.

"Of course. I'll just sit here 'till he walks on in."

"Betty," she said, then paused. "When did you give Ivan a key?"

I hadn't. I knew that. So, naturally, I told her, "He doesn't need a key. He can walk right through the door."

"Oh...I see." She sounded like something was wrong.

"Are you all right, Rosemarie? Everything okay with you and the kids?"

"Oh, of course," she said, too quickly. "Everything's fine. Um, by the way, have you talked to Dr. Jones lately?"

"No, why would I need to?"

"Oh, you know, I mean, it's none of my business, but I thought maybe with the divorce and everything, it couldn't hurt, right?"

She had a point. I thanked her, hung up, and called up Dr. Jones, keeping my eyes on the door the whole time.

One long phone call later, Dr. Jones informed me that I was having what she called a "walking mental breakdown," and that if I didn't check into a private mental hospital before noon tomorrow, she would have me committed.

Rosemarie offered to take me to the hospital, but I refused. I told her, "I'll take myself. I'll have myself committed." She ended up volunteering to pick up the kids instead. Later that day, she pulled into the driveway, hurried the kids into her car, wished me luck, and took them off somewhere. Disneyland, maybe. I wasn't really paying attention.

As I sat there alone with my thoughts, I started wondering: *What does Dr. Jones know?* I could tell for myself if I was crazy or not. All I had to do was summon Ivan with my mind, think about him hard enough, and he would call or show up. In the past it had always worked like a charm. If it worked now, I had nothing to worry about.

I turned off all the lights, left the house, and got in my car. I tuned my mind to think of Ivan and Ivan only. I figured once I came back, I'd see the lights on, because Ivan would be there. I went on a short drive around the neighborhood, and when I came back...the house was still pitch black.

I stopped the car in the middle of the street. *All right,* I thought, *I have a problem.* I asked Dada for a little help putting the house in order, and then, the next morning, I checked myself into a mental hospital.

CHAPTER 22 – MAYBE YOU'RE NOT CRAZY

Memorial Psychiatric Hospital was located in North Hollywood. The morning I checked in, I had on large black sunglasses in the style of Jackie O, an Oleg Cassini navy blue and white suit, and a dark blue leather handbag to match. I walked into the two-story hospital, down a long, cold corridor, and up to the nurses' station. Three middle-aged nurses sat behind an L-shaped counter. I approached the nearest nurse, whose name tag read *Joanna Mitchell.*

I cleared my throat. "Hello, my name is Betty Washington, and I am here to check myself in."

Nurse Joanna took down my name and age, then quickly escorted me to my room. When we walked in, I noticed the window's paisley drapes matched the bedspread on the twin-sized bed. The floor was covered with a green linoleum, and the walls where painted a pale yellow.

As I surveyed the room, the only thing I was grateful for was that I'd been the one to put myself there. The way I understood it, checking myself in meant that I could also check myself out. Dr. Jones had told me over the phone that if she or George were to have me committed, I would need their permission to leave, and my freedom could be lost for good. So that's the thought that kept me going when I got there: *You're free to leave at any time.*

Connected to my bedroom was a bathroom, with a door on each end. Nurse Joanna told me, "You will be sharing this bathroom with the woman across from you, so never lock that door." With that, she invited me to get comfortable and left to let me freshen up.

Which I might have been able to do, if the bathroom hadn't been filthy. The mirror was streaked with spots, the faucet was caked in rust, some kind of yellow gunk was jammed in the drain, and don't get me started on the toilet. Did they expect me to live under those conditions? No way in hell would I put up with that much dirt.

The moment the nurse left, I checked under the sink, found a pair of plastic gloves and a bucket and bleach, and began to clean the toilet. The toilet was my only goal just then – Dr. Jones had always advised me to start small – but wiping it down, taking out all my aggression on that filth and grime, was the best therapy I'd had in years. Before I knew it, I'd polished the whole bathroom to a shine. As I stepped back to admire my work, I looked in the mirror to find the nurse standing right next to me, arms crossed and a look of disapproval on her face.

"Those cleaning supplies shouldn't have been in there," she said. "We can't have our patients running around with bleach."

"What'd you expect me to do?" I asked. "Did you *see* that toilet?"

She dropped her arms and the subject at the same time. "I have something for you," she said, and she took out a capsule and a plastic cup. One drink later, I was out for the night.

I dreamed that Ivan and I were on a small pleasure boat together, sailing across the ocean. Then, all of a sudden, Ivan was in the boat by himself, and I was alone in a leaking rowboat trying to catch up. I paddled as hard as I could, but the faster I worked the oars, the farther away he floated. Finally, I collapsed from exhaustion, and he drifted off as I floated alone, slowly sinking in the middle of the sea.

By the time I woke up, it was nighttime. A nurse I hadn't met yet poked her head in, saw that I was awake, and asked, "Would you care for a bite to eat?" She helped me out of bed and guided me down the hall and around the corner. I heard the clinking of silverware and the murmurs of voices as we approached the hospital's cafeteria.

In short order, I gathered up my dinner and sat across two other women, both of whom looked terrible. Pale, bony and unkempt – they looked bad. On further inspection, just about every woman in the room looked just as bad or worse. No one bothered to comb her hair or put on any type of makeup. All of them looked seriously ill.

Luckily for me, my natural hairstyle was still short, which made it easy to comb and keep presentable. I made it a point to put on my lipstick and powder on my face. I even refused to wear that drab hospital gown that everyone was wearing; instead, I had my turquoise terry cloth dress.

It only took a few days of me coming to the cafeteria in a dress, with my hair and make-up done, before the other ladies began to follow suit. Family members started bringing makeup and casual clothes for them as well. I felt like I'd done something good for them, and whatever else happened, I took some pride in that.

I decided to take more of an interest in befriending the other patients. So when I spotted a short, squatty man, I told him, "Welcome! Let me show you around."

He scowled and told me, "I'm not a patient. I'm the Chief Psychiatrist."

"Oh!" I responded with a chuckle and walked away.

As the days passed, I continued to treat myself in my own way. Before long, I took a liking to walking around the hospital carrying a Bible. I declined to participate in one-on-one therapy. I even opted out of several group sessions. The Chief Psychiatrist held them every day, and I simply walked right past them and headed to my room. I just felt like those sessions were for people who were much, much crazier than I was.

Finally, when I could no longer avoid the mandatory group sessions, I made a late entrance one morning and took my seat. The Chief Psychiatrist couldn't resist prodding me with, "Mrs. Washington! So nice of you to join us." He went on to explain, ostensibly to all of us but mostly to me, that he and the hospital had the power to change our lives.

Having spent most of my free time with the Bible since I got there, I told the doctor, "God has the power! If He wants to destroy this hospital, and you, and everything in it, He can do it. You have no power. Nothing! God has all the power, and God will surely punish you, and I don't plan to be here in this room when he brings His wrath upon you!" It seemed like the right thing to say at the time.

Dr. Jones, who was working one-on-one with me (or trying to), seemed irritated with my behavior. She increased my lithium medication, and I began to sleep even more. My dreams with Ivan became a regular occurrence. The dreams were different, but the theme was always the same. I'd always start out with Ivan, get pulled away from him somehow, try to get back to him, and fail. The last one I remember took place on that same cliff; we danced, I fell, I hit the rocks, and then...nothing but blackness. I was sleeping for twelve hours at a stretch most days, and every time, I hated the way I felt when I woke up.

In my waking hours, my muscles felt weak, I had excessive urination, and my speech sometimes slurred and ran together as I chatted with the other female patients.

I decided I didn't need the medication. I would just hide it under my tongue and pretend to swallow it in front of the nurse; then, when she left, I would spit in the toilet and flush it away.

After a couple of weeks there, I started gaining weight and feeling normal again. My dreams with Ivan gradually stopped, and calmness came over my being.

I still missed Ivan, but his not being in my life was starting to make sense, and I knew it was for the best all around.

One morning, I woke up and had an urge to go see a movie. Back when we were together, Ivan and I would see a movie at least once a week, and I was missing that routine in my life. I walked up to my nurse and said, "I would like a pass to go see a movie in Hollywood."

My nurse granted the pass. It was 6:00 pm, right after they'd served us our last meal of the day. Eager for my one evening of freedom, I swiftly headed out to my car. With each step, the thought of Ivan danced in my head. That thought led me to remember that he still had one of my sociology books, as well as a large professional photograph of myself. I decided to go get my belongings, so I forgot about my outing to Hollywood and headed for Altadena instead.

I had only been to Altadena once, so I wasn't sure exactly where I was going. By the time I reached Ivan's neighborhood, night was upon me. I headed down a few local streets before turning onto one that looked familiar. To my surprise, I had no problem remembering where Ivan's house was.

I carefully stepped out of my car and stood in front of his house, soaking in all the memories. Then I proceeded up the walkway and approached the front door. My heart began to race. It had been over a month since I'd seen his wife, and longer than that since I'd seen Ivan himself.

I rang the bell and stood still as a statue as his wife opened the door. The moment Berlie saw me, she ran from the open door and came back with a plate of ice cubes to throw at me. Staying calm, I told her firmly, "You only get one chance to hit me. So make sure you get a good shot. I'm here for my textbook and my photograph. That's all."

She quietly lowered the ice. As she stood there and glared at me, Ivan walked up to the door. "Bette," he said, with surprise plain to see in his smile, "please, come in."

I looked deep into Ivan's brown eyes. I wanted to jump into his arms and let all my worries wash away. Instead, I stood strong and said, "No, I only want my textbook and photograph."

Ivan and I held a stare, packed with volumes of thoughts and feelings. Our trance was broken when we heard his wife scream, "Maybe you're not crazy, but the two of you are trying to make *me* crazy!"

I redirected my eyes towards Ivan and calmly said, "No, I'm not crazy. You're right. I just want my things."

Ivan turned, went into his home, and came back with my book and photograph.

His wife was still standing there, looking a bit deranged as she watched Ivan bring up my belongings. She told me, "You know, he has your photograph at work too, so he can look at you all day!" She shook her head, hissed, and told us both, "Say what you have to say here." Then she stomped off down the hall, and I heard a door slam.

The slam didn't even break Ivan's gaze on me. "Please, Bette," he said, "won't you come in?"

"No," I told him, keeping my voice as level as possible. "That's not what I came here for." Of course, my reasons for being there had nothing to do with any book or photograph." What I needed was to see Ivan, to see his face, connect with his soul one last time before I walked away for good.

Ivan handed me my belongings. I told him, "Thank you," took my textbook and photograph, and walked away from the door.

As I headed back down his walkway and toward the quiet Altadena street, I swear I heard Ivan say, "Bette, wait, don't go. I love you."

I choked back my feelings along with my tears. I didn't break my stride. Not until I got to the end of his walkway and into my car. I drove a few feet, but had to pull over when my emotions found their way out of my valley and overpowered me. Alone at the wheel by the side of the road, I wept uncontrollably.

Then I felt a surge of warm, soft energy engulf every part of my being, and I knew I was free... free. I took a deep, cleansing breath as I continued down the street, never once looking back.

The ride back to the hospital seemed to take a lifetime. *I saw Ivan again. I'll never see him again.* Back and forth, back and forth for the entire drive.

Some people are brought into our lives for a season, a reason, or a lifetime. I had to come to grips with that, and somehow, I had to put Ivan in the "reason" category. What I came to understand was that God wanted me to know what it felt like to love and to be loved. I could say beyond a doubt I'd learned that with Ivan, however short it may have been.

At a red light, I clutched my sociology textbook and stared at the photograph of myself. It was a timeless professional color portrait. I was dressed in a black and white polka-dot dress. The organza silk fabric gracefully adorned my shoulders. My hair was in a fresh natural cut, and I wore a thin shade of coral lipstick. Ivan had loved this picture. He'd called it "regal."

As I stared in the eyes of that woman in the portrait, I saw something in her I hadn't before. She had a certain softness, a tenderness to her gaze. In her hands, I saw strength – even when they shook, even when they let go, *strength*. I held that portrait close to my chest, and only in the back of my mind did I think, *This is as close as you'll ever get to Ivan again.*

I gazed out the window as I headed back to my temporary residence. I couldn't help but wonder what was going through Ivan's mind at that very moment. Then I pushed that question away. *Stay present,* I told myself. I had said goodbye to my soulmate for the very last time, and that was that.

When I walked back into the hospital, Nurse Joanna ran up to me in a panic. "Call your doctor immediately," she said. I headed to the pay phone in the hallway and dialed Dr. Jones' number.

She picked up the phone and started to laugh when she heard my voice. She asked, "How did you like your trip to Altadena?"

Before I could ask her how she knew, she continued, "Ivan called me. You scared the hell out of him. I assured him you're not dangerous. He wanted to know if I knew you were out."

"What did you tell him?"

"I told him I'd given you permission to see a movie in Hollywood. Obviously, you changed your mind," said Dr. Jones.

"Scared the hell out of him," had I? I'd wondered how he might take my surprise visit. Now I knew.

The doctor continued, "I also told him that you were getting much better, and that you were in no way psychotic."

"Thanks." I hung up the phone and headed to my room. Exhausted as I was, I had just enough energy left to put my textbook and photograph in a safe place before I laid down on my bed and fell into another deep sleep – without my medication this time.

Later, I found out that George and Ivan had spoken with each other and discussed coming together to the hospital. They'd agreed to work together to help me get well. Dr. Jones had talked them out of it, and in fact told them both to leave me alone, saying they were the reason I was there in the first place.

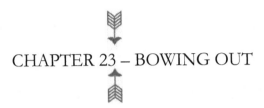

CHAPTER 23 – BOWING OUT

I spent my next several days at the hospital planning a party.

With George out of my life, I was bowing out of society, and I'd decided the news of our divorce would not be heard through the grapevine, but instead through me. This was a long time coming and a hard road traveled, but I felt that I'd arrived, finally pulling through some of the hardest times of my life.

I planned out my guest list carefully, only inviting people that had made a special impact in my life and represented a positive force. I hired a caterer from the mental hospital and charged everything to Dr. Washington. I decided to host a formal sit-down dinner for, oh, fifty people, I wasn't shy in ordering the best of the best for the affair, either; my menu had everything from shrimp cocktail to prime-cut steak and fresh lobster. I even added some heavenly champagne to top it off.

The total came out to over two thousand dollars. I'd always used that same caterer, so nobody asked any questions when I had the bill sent to Dr.

Washington. I figured this was the least he could do to pay me back for all the shit he'd put me through.

In no time, everything came together, and my party was a success.

The next day after my party at the hospital, I discovered the charge for my stay was seventy-five dollars per day. The moment I came to that realization, I checked myself out. While I was packing my bags and saying goodbye to some friends I'd made there, my doctor called and told me that I could leave…but not go home. I missed my kids terribly, but she said I wasn't well enough to take care of three children.

So, after a two-and-a-half-week stay, I headed out of the mental hospital and immediately checked myself into the first affordable LA motel I saw. The bright afternoon made me realize how much I'd missed the sun's warmth on my skin. After a quick walk and a cheap meal, I decided to ignore the doctor, head straight home, and see my children again.

I felt wonderful in body and mind. Where Ivan had once occupied my every waking thought, he now made only occasional cameos. After settling back in with Dada and the kids, I felt up for a nice beauty treatment, and headed straight for Jan's Beauty Salon.

At the salon, I heard an odd bit of gossip: Sidney Poitier had been talking to Ivan about me. Apparently, Ivan owed Sidney some kind of debt, and Sidney offered to clear it if Ivan would let me go and rebuild his relationship with his wife.

As soon as I heard that, I took an unplanned trip over to Sidney's house. When he opened the door, I didn't even give him a chance to speak before blurting out, "Why are you interfering with Ivan and me?"

Sidney just looked at me, probably wondering what had possessed me to walk right up to his front door and ring his bell. In hindsight, I wonder the same thing. He politely invited me inside, but I refused. "Betty," he said, "I've always thought you were a very kind and beautiful lady."

"Well, this kind and beautiful lady is fighting for her sanity. Stay out of our business." I turned and left without giving him the opportunity to respond.

Two weeks after being home, I decided to have a small get-together, with just my girlfriends. At the party, a few friends mentioned to me that they were taking trips abroad. My good friend Mary Lou Broussard was going to Madrid to study Spanish. My other friend Lovey Wilson was taking a trip to Paris. I'd never really thought about going outside of the country, but the suggestion couldn't have come at a better time. I thought to myself, *I'll go to Europe too.*

I'd never learned much about world travel, and so I had no idea I couldn't leave the US without a passport. My friend Bob Rogers had to take me down to the Federal Building that Monday. He explained the whole process, talked me through all the pictures and paperwork, and seven days later, my express passport arrived.

I didn't have much of a clue about airfare either; in fact, I'd started planning this whole trip without any idea how to pay for any of it. Luckily, George came through for once; maybe he just wanted me gone for a while, or maybe he really did care, but either way, he put up the money for the trip on his own accord.

My next hurdle was the need to provide good care for my children. My nanny, who could not stay overnight, overheard me mentioning to one of the ladies that I was thinking of going to Europe for a few weeks in the summer. She recommended splitting the work with her granddaughter, who was a college graduate and needed a summer job. I asked her granddaughter to live in my home and take care of my kids for two weeks while I went abroad. That decision was hard for me to make, but she was a grown adult, her work as an English teacher in Mexico gave her experience with children, and my kids would still have Dada their regular nanny; all of that made the verdict a bit easier.

I filled the fridge and freezer. I also left my car and gas card so the babysitter could take the children out to the playground or the beach. That left only one thing to do before I took off. I picked up the phone to tell George I was going.

He was silent for a moment, then said, "I was just talking to Ivan, and Ivan said—"

"Stop," I told him. "Stop. Please stop. I don't want to hear about your conversation with Ivan." I wanted nothing to do with anything from my mental breakdown, not then, not ever. I hung up the phone and started packing for my trip to Europe.

I felt the old tingly feeling, the one that always crept up on me when I took a step into the unknown. I couldn't wait to take another step, and another, until all my troubles were thousands of miles away.

Whenever Ivan or George popped in my head, I would shoo them away immediately. Oftentimes, I found myself recalling a film Ivan and I went to see when we were dating, Fellini's film *Juliet of the Spirits*. It was all about the visions, memories, and mysticism that help a 40-something woman find the strength to leave her cheating husband.

Ivan and I saw a lot of movies together, but I never forgot that one. As I ran the movie over in my head, I realized how much I wanted and needed to be free – not only from George, but from both of them. In the movie's last scene, Juliet is hanging clothes on a line, alone in the pleasant breeze, and that simple scene beautifully conveys how free she's become from all the madness around her. The more I recalled that scene, the more it felt as if her spirit jumped out of the screen and became a part of mine.

Now, just like her, I was free. Free from George's indifference. Free from Ivan's indecision. Free from Berlie's jealousy. Free from adultery and judgment and chaos and fear. Most of all, free to love myself.

I believe God had a hand in granting me that freedom. I believe He does things to protect His children, and one of those things was to remove Ivan and George from my head to ease the pain of losing them.

Two nights after my passport arrived, I was on the freeway doing 90 miles an hour to LAX. *A season, a reason, or a lifetime.* I kept replaying that in my head. Yes, Ivan had definitely been a "reason," but he was past now, and I resolved to take what I experienced with him and let it propel me to my future, to the next chapter of my life, whatever that might be.

I was headed for Europe. I had $300.00, three blank checks, and the Diner's Club credit card my attorney Matthews had eventually gotten back from George. I left the rest of the checks in a locker at the airport. No reservations anywhere. I didn't know a soul in Europe, but that's where I was headed. Was I crazy? Yes, I was, and I had the Lithium pills in my purse to prove it.

As I walked toward the terminal, a heavy thought seeped through the mist of all my craziness, and that thought was: *You only live once, and each day, you move closer to not being here.* I needed to live and see the world; I needed to get out of Los Angeles and away from my manic life, period. I knew I had to grow stronger for my children, for me, for our future together. So there I was, in the midst of a breakdown and a life change all rolled up in one.

I took a deep breath, then stepped onto that turbo jet.

I don't regret a single step of that dance on the cliff, with all its thrills and love and terror. I fell, and I took that fall, but I missed the rocks and hit the water. I swam, and I climbed, and when I found my partner still up at the top of the cliff, I squeezed his hand and walked away, forever grateful for the dance of a lifetime.

THE END

Mother and daughter, co-authors, Fatima and Bettina Washington

ABOUT THE AUTHOR

Bettina E. Washington is a retired educator with Oakland Public Schools, boasting 28 years of dedicated service and leadership. She is the mother of four children and a member of the Alpha Kappa Alpha sorority.

She is a world traveler, having crossing the Atlantic Ocean over 35 times so far. Her favorite destinations are Rome, Israel, and Paris.

At the vibrant age of 82, Ms. Washington completed her first non-fiction work. *The Cliff Dancer: My Love Affair with Ivan Dixon* is the first of three planned books about passionate self-discovery and the triumph of a woman's spirit.

The book has been written in collaboration with her youngest daughter, Fatima Washington, a filmmaker and educator in Los Angeles.

Made in the USA
Charleston, SC
13 October 2015